Tim P. VanDuivendyk, DMin

The Unwanted Gift
of Grief
A Ministry Approach

Pre-publication
REVIEWS,
COMMENTARIES,
EVALUATIONS . . .

"This book is one of the most comprehensive guides to grieving and to walking with the grieving that is available today. The physical, mental, relational, and spiritual dimensions are all considered in balance and in depth. It is unusual in its sensitivity to the faith and religious dimensions of the griever. It balances well theoretical, practical, personal, and storied perspectives on the grief journey. I will use this rich resource for teaching seminarians, chaplain students, and congregational care providers."

Steven S. Ivy, MDiv, PhD
Senior Vice President,
Values, Ethics, Social Responsibility,
and Pastoral Services
Clarian Health Partners

"There are aspects of grief and loss that are often overlooked in our culture of narcissism. Americans are programmed from childhood to seek happiness without loss, and love without grief. In *The Unwanted Gift of Grief*, counselor Tim P. VanDuivendyk has provided a window for viewing every conceivable aspect of loss and grief work. He addresses persons who experience losses in life and those who sojourn alongside them with his wisdom gained from many years of therapeutic work with wounded people. This book offers Christian hope and consolation to sufferers and their supportive sojourners."

C. W. Brister
Distinguished Professor Emeritus
of Pastoral Ministry,
Southwestern Baptist Theological
Seminary

More pre-publication
REVIEWS, COMMENTARIES, EVALUATIONS . . .

"Think everything that can be said about grief is already written? Not so. VanDuivendyk's personal experiences with grief, plus decades of service as a hospital chaplain, a licensed professional counselor, and a marriage and family therapist, enable him to view the subject from a unique perspective.

The author's view is that grief, though terribly painful, is a *gift* to be accepted over time. Without arguing for a pet theory about recovery, he shows how the process is unique to every mourner. The numerous practical suggestions will inform both those overwhelmed by loss and those who care for the grieving—whom he calls sojourners. The chapter on anger and frustration, even at God, and the attention to the impact of grief on marriage are issues that most authors neglect. VanDuivendyk avoids technical/academic jargon so the book is easy to understand. This book will be particularly meaningful to Christians who struggle with the faith aspects of loss. Out of his own encounters with God, the author deals insightfully with feeling abandoned by God, being angry at God, and the desire to pray for miracles."

Andrew D. Lester, PhD
Emeritus Professor of Pastoral Theology
and Pastoral Counseling,
Brite Divinity School,
Texas Christian University

"This sensitive, compassionate, and knowledgeable response to grief reads as if one were sitting on the couch in the author's office, so personal is the approach. Clearly, here is a master who has himself made the journey through the gratitude of grief, the wilderness of despair, and come to the healing light that differentiating brings. It is a must for ministry groups who want to sojourn with those on the grief wilderness path. The practical guide for couples is a unique offering to those who are lost in the grief wilderness and are searching to find a way.

The uniqueness of each person's response to grief is the core concept of the book and helps those who feel alone to know that they own their response and it is the valid expression of grief for them. The book helps us understand the differentiating that must transpire for us to move onward with a secure self in spite of our loss. The author helps us see this as the movement of truth in moving out of the shadows that come with grief. It is as we incorporate loss into life we are able to build a new path."

Gwen Sherwood, RN, PhD, FAAN
Professor and Associate Dean
for Academic Affairs,
The University of North Carolina
at Chapel Hill

"The time we live in requires that we live with a knowledge of death that helps us celebrate life. This book guides us in this direction. To celebrate life we must learn to honor death. The author takes us by the hand and walks us through this process. This book is as real as death itself. A must read."

Pat Love, EdD
Pat Love & Associates, Austin, Texas;
Author of *The Emotional Incest Syndrome*;
Columnist; Speaker

"This book has certainly been a ministry to me. Dr. VanDuivendyk provides a theologically sound and practical approach to dealing with one of life's most difficult and complex issues. Grief is a tough wilderness journey, and this book is invaluable in helping one navigate through it. The final chapter has extraordinary significance for me. The author used many of these ideas as he counseled me following the tragic death of my wife. His spiritual ideas guided me to a wholesome—and continuing—recovery."

Dan S. Wilford, MHA
President (Retired), Memorial Hermann Healthcare System

"In this book, VanDuivendyk has developed a way to teach health professionals about grief and the individual's response stages which progressively peels the layers away, and has almost a rhythmic regularity to the progressive discoveries. Each chapter almost stands alone, yet it clearly bridges from the previous to the next like verses of a compelling ballad. We honor the beloved departed by the depth of our grief. That depth of grief and how we reconstruct our lives afterward can be tools to forge a marvelously positive memorial. This book provides the structured learning required by most health professionals to conscientiously care for their patients and clients in grief. It helps make wise, knowing, and unfearful physicians, psychiatrists, social workers, clergy, pastoral caregivers, school grief counselors, violence victim counselors, and others, who must become listening, caring, and equipping sojourners with each person in grief. It should stand beside *A Grief Observed* (C. S. Lewis) as the map or guideline to the stages of passionate grief and its recovery."

Elisabeth McSherry, MD, MPH
National Consultant to Veterans Administration Chaplaincy

More pre-publication
REVIEWS, COMMENTARIES, EVALUATIONS . . .

"It is a rare and valuable book which manages to helpfully address grief both for the bereaved and for their caregivers. I have had the unwanted opportunity to consider this clear, thoughtful work from both perspectives; I read it on the way to and from the burial of my friend of thirty-two years. The author's insights into the meaning of grief and his clarity about the different ways people grieve were particularly helpful. I read this book as I was considering the curriculum for my students, and the contributions this material has for beginners in spiritual care are crystal clear. One student asked to be allowed to take the book home so he could finish reading it that night—an eloquent statement of its immediacy. The author's deep Christian faith resonates throughout and brings light to many of the corners of grief from which we all too often wish to turn away from. He has made a richly personal and professional contribution to our field."

Chaplain Arthur M. Lucas, MDiv, BCC
Director, Spiritual Care/Palliative Care/Interpreter Services, Barnes-Jewish Hospital, St. Louis, Missouri

"I very much enjoyed this book. The author has clearly laid out his approach and presented it in very manageable segments which will appeal to chaplains, local clergy, and especially Christian lay people. The author strikes an excellent balance between theory and practice. I particularly liked the practical aspect of this book where caregivers are offered specific guidelines in their 'sojourning' process with parishioners, patients, and families. The author is not afraid of the most difficult feelings connected with grief work—anger, rage, depression—both in himself and in his readers.

VanDuivendyk brings substantial knowledge to this subject from the fields of family systems, human development, psychology, and clinical supervision. He writes in an accessible way that will be very appealing to the general reader. Though much of the territory he covers is familiar, he gives the material a freshness and focus which is extremely helpful."

Joan E. Hemenway, DMin
President, Association for Clinical Pastoral Education

The Haworth Pastoral Press®
An Imprint of The Haworth Press, Inc.
New York • London • Oxford

The Unwanted Gift
of Grief
A Ministry Approach

THE HAWORTH PASTORAL PRESS®
Religion and Mental Health
Harold G. Koenig, MD
Senior Editor

A Theology of God-Talk: The Language of the Heart by J. Timothy Allen

A Practical Guide to Hospital Ministry: Healing Ways by Junietta B. McCall

Pastoral Care for Post-Traumatic Stress Disorder: Healing the Shattered Soul by Daléne Fuller Rogers

Integrating Spirit and Psyche: Using Women's Narratives in Psychotherapy by Mary Pat Henehan

Chronic Pain: Biomedical and Spiritual Approaches by Harold G. Koenig

Spirituality in Pastoral Counseling and the Community Helping Professions by Charles Topper

Parish Nursing: A Handbook for the New Millennium edited by Sybil D. Smith

Mental Illness and Psychiatric Treatment: A Guide for Pastoral Counselors by Gregory B. Collins and Thomas Culbertson

The Power of Spirituality in Therapy: Integrating Spiritual and Religious Beliefs in Mental Health Practice by Peter A. Kahle and John M. Robbins

Bereavement Counseling: Pastoral Care for Complicated Grieving by Junietta Baker McCall

Biblical Stories for Psychotherapy and Counseling: A Sourcebook by Matthew B. Schwartz and Kalman J. Kaplan

A Christian Approach to Overcoming Disability: A Doctor's Story by Elaine Leong Eng

Faith, Medicine, and Science: A Festschrift in Honor of Dr. David B. Larson edited by Jeff Levin and Harold G. Koenig

Encyclopedia of Ageism by Erdman Palmore, Laurence Branch, and Diana Harris

Dealing with the Psychological and Spiritual Aspects of Menopause: Finding Hope in the Midlife by Dana E. King, Melissa H. Hunter, and Jerri R. Harris

Spirituality and Mental Health: Clinical Applications by Gary W. Hartz

Dying Declarations: Notes from a Hospice Volunteer by David B. Resnik

Maltreatment of Patients in Nursing Homes: There Is No Safe Place by Diana K. Harris and Michael L. Benson

Is There a God in Health Care? Toward a New Spirituality of Medicine by William F. Haynes and Geffrey B. Kelly

Guide to Ministering to Alzheimer's Patients and Their Families by Patricia A. Otwell

The Unwanted Gift of Grief: A Ministry Approach by Tim P. Van Duivendyk

The Treatment of Bipolar Disorder in Pastoral Counseling: Community and Silence edited by David Welton

The Unwanted Gift
of Grief
A Ministry Approach

Tim P. VanDuivendyk, DMin

The Haworth Pastoral Press®
An Imprint of The Haworth Press, Inc.
New York • London • Oxford

For more information on this book or to order, visit
http://www.haworthpress.com/store/product.asp?sku=5644

or call 1-800-HAWORTH (800-429-6784) in the United States and Canada
or (607) 722-5857 outside the United States and Canada

or contact orders@HaworthPress.com

Published by

The Haworth Pastoral Press®, an imprint of The Haworth Press, Inc., 10 Alice Street, Binghamton,
NY 13904-1580.

PUBLISHER'S NOTE
The development, preparation, and publication of this work has been undertaken with great care.
However, the Publisher, employees, editors, and agents of The Haworth Press are not responsible
for any errors contained herein or for consequences that may ensue from use of materials or
information contained in this work. The Haworth Press is committed to the dissemination of ideas
and information according to the highest standards of intellectual freedom and the free exchange of
ideas. Statements made and opinions expressed in this publication do not necessarily reflect
the views of the Publisher, Directors, management, or staff of The Haworth Press, Inc., or an
endorsement by them.

Identities and circumstances of individuals discussed in this book have been changed to protect
confidentiality.

Cover photo by John Lynch.

Cover design by Marylouise E. Doyle.

Library of Congress Cataloging-in-Publication Data

VanDuivendyk, Tim P.
    The unwanted gift of grief : a ministry approach / Tim P. VanDuivendyk.
        p. cm.
    Includes bibliographical references and index.
    ISBN-13: 978-0-7890-2949-2 (hc. : alk. paper)
    ISBN-10: 0-7890-2949-9 (hc. : alk. paper)
    ISBN-13: 978-0-7890-2950-8 (pbk. : alk. paper)
    ISBN-10: 0-7890-2950-2 (pbk. : alk. paper)
    1. Grief—Religious aspects—Christianity. 2. Pastoral counseling. I. Title.

BV4905.3.V38 2006
259'.6—dc22

                                                                    2005034443

To Jeanne: my friend, encourager, wife
fellow sojourner in love, grief, and transformation . . .
God's graceful and grace-filled gift.

ABOUT THE AUTHOR

Tim P. VanDuivendyk, DMin, MDiv, BS, is Chaplain and Assistant Vice President of Spiritual Care and Development at Memorial Hermann Healthcare System in Houston, Texas. He is certified with the Association for Clinical Pastoral Education, Inc., the Association of Professional Chaplains, and is a licensed professional counselor and licensed marriage and family therapist in the state of Texas. His work has appeared in *Parish Nurses, Health Care Chaplains and Community Clergy: Navigating the Maze of Professional Relationships* (Haworth), and the *Journal of Health Care Chaplaincy* (Haworth).

CONTENTS

Foreword   **xi**

        John R. Claypool

Acknowledgments   **xiii**

Introduction   **1**

  Overview of the Book   5

PART I: THE UNWANTED GIFT

Chapter 1. Grief As Gratitude, Grief As Gift   **9**

  The Wilderness of Grief: The "Way" to Transformation   9
  Without Facing the Pain, Growth May Be Limited   14
  Letting Go of the Past, We Rise to New Life   15
  Grief: A Journey of Wondering and Wandering
    in the Wilderness   17

Chapter 2. Everyone Grieves Differently   **19**

  How Long Will I Grieve?   20
  The Effects of Family and Culture on Grieving   22
  Different Pathways Through Grief: Think People,
    Feel People, and Act People   24
  Introverts and Extroverts   30

Chapter 3. Factors That Affect the Wilderness of Grief   **33**

  The Faith Factor   33
  The Need for Sojourners: Counselors, Ministers, and Friends   37
  Sudden Loss or Slow, Unfolding Loss   39
  Rejection and Suicide   40
  The Life Cycle and Development   45
  Differentiation and Enmeshment   46

PART II: THE WILDERNESS OF GRIEF

Chapter 4. Unbelievable Darkness   **55**

The Dynamics of Darkness   55
Types of Shock and Disbelief   56
Temporary or Permanent Amnesia   61

Chapter 5. Frustration and Anger Amid "Why?"   **65**

Frustration and Anger: Part of the Journey   66
Frustration and Anger As Regret, Remorse, or Guilt   68
Frustration and Anger Toward Others   71

Chapter 6. Praying for a Miracle   **81**

Holy and Earthly Contracts: Hope for Healing and Cure   82
Miracles and Saying "Yes" to Death and Suffering   84
Mom's Good Death   92
Advance Directives and DNR Orders   94
Abby's Good Miracle   94

Chapter 7. Wrestling with Sadness and Depression   **101**

Sadness and Depression: Normal Parts of Healing   101
Movement into Light and Healing   108
Signs of When Depression Is Too Deep   110
Getting Help: When, What, and Where   113

Chapter 8. Healing: Experiencing the Light Again   **115**

Turning Points in the Wilderness   116
Caution: Euphoria May Be Ahead!   118
What Does This Healing Transformation Look or Feel
Like?   120
What Is This Mysterious Spirit That Transforms Us
Through the Wilderness?   126

Chapter 9. And Yet . . . We Never Forget!   **129**

The Return of Grief: "Peek-a-Boo" Experiences   129

PART III: SOJOURNERS IN THE WILDERNESS— HOW TO HELP

Chapter 10. Being a Sojourner   **137**

What Is a Sojourner?   137
Appendix: The Sojourner Process Guide—Walking
    with Another Through the Wilderness of Grief   140

Chapter 11. Sojourning with Those in Unbelievable Darkness   **143**

Chapter 12. Sojourning with Those Frustrated and Angry Amid "Why?"   **147**

Chapter 13. Sojourning with Those Praying for a Miracle   **153**

Chapter 14. Sojourning with Those Wrestling with Sadness and Depression   **159**

Chapter 15. Sojourning with Those in Healing and Light   **163**

PART IV: MORE WAYS TOWARD TRANSFORMATION

Chapter 16. Marriage: Tough Enough Without Grief   **169**

Couples and Grieving   169
Gender Differences and Grieving   171
Complementarity in Marriage and Grief   174
The Gift of Sexual Closeness Amid Grief   175
Appendix: The Grief Date—A Guide for Couples
    and Family Members   176

Chapter 17. Ways of Making it Through the Wilderness of Grief   **179**

Notes   **185**

Suggested Reading   **187**

Index   **189**

Foreword

In this era of increasing specialization, it is rare indeed to find an author who is well-versed in a variety of discipline simultaneously. Dr. Tim VanDuivendyk is just such a person. For over thirty years, he has patiently and diligently invested his energies in a variety of areas. He is an ordained minister, a highly credentialed personal counselor, an administrator of a pastoral care program in a large urban hospital system, and a frequent lecturer to both professional and lay groups. In addition to what all of these roles have contributed to his understanding, he is also a husband and a father who knows firsthand what issues are evoked when genuine grief casts its shadow across the human pathway. I think this latter "credential" is what gives such power to the words that he writes. It is one thing to compile information and construct theories about a given subject. It is quite another to put into action what one has only previously thought about abstractly. Dr. VanDuivendyk is a veteran of both of these processes, which means that his insights have been tested through personal experiences and, thus, have the potency to speak home to the heart as well as the mind.

The following pages will enlighten even the most learned professional about the reality of grief and the many ways of responding to such an awesome trauma. At the same time, those people whose only competence is simply finding themselves in the unwanted valley of the shadow of loss can profit genuinely by reading these words. The title of this work is appropriately paradoxical, for who initially would think of linking the words "grief" and "gift" in the same sentence? However, I find this the unique quality of VanDuivendyk's work. This is not a book of one-sided, simplistic platitudes. The author is as honest about the inherent darkness of grief and the inevitable struggles that such an experience evokes as he is about the hope that lies buried in the broken pieces of the way it was. This hope, and several very

The Unwanted Gift of Grief: A Ministry Approach
© 2006 by The Haworth Press, Inc. All rights reserved.
doi:10.1300/5644_a

original and creative ways of getting in touch with this life-sustaining reality, are what give this book such a healing potential for all who carefully give themselves to the reading and "inwardly digesting" of what Dr. VanDuivendyk so generously shares.

I am personally delighted that such a labor of love and learning is new being made available in this new form. The author has touched countless lives as a minister, counselor, and speaker. Now this same gift enters the mystery of the written word that can get to more places than he could ever go in person. I predict that such an enlargement of influence will multiply the redemptive blessing that has already emanated from the life of this good man.

John R. Claypool, PhD
Episcopal minister
Professor of Homiletics
McAffee School of Theology
Mercer University
author, Tracks of
a Fellow Struggle

Acknowledgments

Moving through grief to transformation is learned by sojourning through one's own losses and by sojourning with others through their losses. I have been painfully blessed to experience both of these gifts. The stories in this book are not only about my personal grief, but also about grief in the lives of others.

As a hospital chaplain with Memorial Hermann Healthcare System and as an individual, marriage, and family therapist, many have invited me to sojourn with them in the wilderness of suffering and loss. They have taught me much about pain, suffering, the age-old truth that it rains on the just and the unjust, and the faith to transform toward new life after a loss or extreme disappointment.

Fellow human beings are powerful teachers. I hope I have been a good student and listened well. I am grateful for, honored by, and humbled by all who have invited me to walk grief's sacred journey with them. They have modeled for me the spiritual labor and contractions between hope and despair, faith and doubt, and courage and fear that give birth to new life. They will never know how they have touched my life with their trust, courage, faith, and hope.

Abby, my daughter, has been one of those teachers. Abby was born with a mental and physical challenge known as Down syndrome. You will get to know how she has taught me in the pages ahead. Abby has a spirit that bends but never breaks.

Throughout my ministry, I have taught ministry interns, residents, and seminarians in clinical pastoral education and spoken at community seminars and congregations. They have graciously encouraged me to write. Vernon and Yvonne Garrett offered their lake house as a peaceful place to renew my spirit and write. I have no idea how they could think about me, while they were feeling overwhelmed with the loss of a young son to a massive heart attack. These are gifts I can never repay, but hopefully can pass on to others.

The Unwanted Gift of Grief: A Ministry Approach
© 2006 by The Haworth Press, Inc. All rights reserved.
doi:10.1300/5644_b

Even my crazy fishing buddies have taught me. For more than twenty years we have gone fishing together in order to have a manly excuse to share stories, laughter, and tears. We have supported each other through numerous losses and tough times. We have had much to celebrate and laugh about over the years, in spite of catching very few fish. I have always said that those who grieve deeply also laugh deeply. We do both profoundly.

When I reflect on those who have been my significant grief educators, the list is long. It is impossible to name everyone.

I am deeply blessed by John R. Claypool's words in the Foreword, written just months before his death. John was a spiritual giant of our time. He blessed and influenced me and others with his grace-filled personhood, confessional preaching style, and soul-searching classic book, *Tracks of a Fellow Struggler.* Although shadows of struggle and grief often interfaced his pilgrimage, John went into and through the unwanted wilderness of grief and found gift and gratitude. Not afraid to name and search his painful narrative, he taught us to name and search our own.

My professors and professional mentors have been Donald Bratton, ThM, C.W. Brister, PhD, Frank Chesky, MD, John Claypool, PhD, Thomas Cole, ThM, George Gaston III, PhD, Robert Grigsby, MDiv, Jerry Humble, MSW, Pat Love, EdD, Robert Mulkey, MDiv, Jim Ranton, DMin, Deborah Whisnand, ThM, and unnamed others who have touched my ministry.

Treasured fellow sojourners have shared their wilderness stories, modeled transformation, or have closely coached this manuscript. I want to gratefully name a few: Debbie and Kirk Brassfield, Bill Davis, ThM, Yvonne Garrett, MA, Carol Gay, MS, Genie Hawkins, Scott Hendry, MDiv, Janet Mayo, Susan Nance, ThM, Lynette Guy Ranton, JD, LeeAnn Nolan Rathbun, MDiv, Mauricio Reinoso, MD, Paul Robertson, PhD, Robert Scraper, MBA, Renea Schumann, PhD, RN, Gwen Sherwood, PhD, RN, Cyd Thomas, MDiv, Jeff Tomkins, MS, Julie Tomkins, MA, Patricia Tooley, BSN, RN, Peggy Tyner, MA, John Unger, MA, Abby VanDuivendyk, Erik VanDuivendyk, MS, Sherian and Phil VanDuivendyk, Dan Wilford, MHA, Jeanne Tomkins VanDuivendyk, and others beyond the grasp of my eight-year memory while writing this manuscript.

For my chaplain colleagues at Memorial Hermann and the hundreds of chaplain residents who have trained at Memorial Hermann,

I say thank you. For more than thirty years you have listened to me pontificate about loss and grief and still stayed awake to offer discussion and feedback. What a gift!

My family has shaped me and taught me in so many ways I cannot fully name. Our children, Abby, Erik, Jeff, and Julie, have known the wilderness of grief. Each managed and transformed through divorce or death of parents. I am grateful for each of them. Each has grieved differently and for different reasons. Now as adults they continue to teach me how to move toward transformation, growth, and fulfillment.

Especially am I grateful for Jeanne, my graceful and grace-filled wife. She has been a tender encourager, colleague, and sojourner in grief and also a soul mate in joy and love. We both have known grief through death and divorce years ago. Working through our losses, we put together new life, love, marriage, and family. Jeanne knows the wilderness of loss, grief, and transformation.

Introduction

Since the night my daughter was born more than thirty years ago, this book has been welling up within me. Abby was born with a mental and physical challenge called Down syndrome. The feelings of shock, confusion, disappointment, injustice, anger, and sadness were intense for a couple of years. Still today, as I love and enjoy her, grief seeps to the surface when I least expect it. Yet, Abby has been a great teacher when it comes to sorrow and grief, but also a great teacher of courage and joy. She is a delightful gift of unconditional pure love.

This book is written for those in the midst of loss and grief and those who want to help someone in the midst of loss and grief. It is also for the one who has never known grief but wants to better understand its journey, dynamics, and process. The pages ahead will invite you into the unwanted gift of grief. This gift can lead to transformation, growth, and healing, but "yes" it is a painful wilderness journey.

All of us are touched by grief in some way. From extreme disappointment to death, the causes for grief are many. Some deaths we may call "a good death." This may be a parent who lived a long and fulfilling life. Along with celebration and gratitude for their lives, we also grieve. The emotions related to "a good death" may be strong or subtle. Some deaths will never be considered "a good death." Some losses will never be subtle but rather they devastate our lives and shake our souls. You have known grief or someone around you who has grieved.

- A neighbor's husband suffered a fatal heart attack. What can we say or do?
- Thousands were killed by terrorist attack at the World Trade Center in New York City. After a few months most went on with our lives, while families continued to grieve intensely for years, even to this day. How long can we support them?

The Unwanted Gift of Grief: A Ministry Approach
© 2006 by The Haworth Press, Inc. All rights reserved.
doi:10.1300/5644_01

1

- A CEO of a large health care system finally retired and was ready to play, relax, and be with family more. On one of many trips to visit children and grandchildren, he and his wife were in a fatal vehicle accident. She was killed instantly and his injuries were treated for months. How do we make it through sudden trauma and loss?
- A finance executive was diagnosed with cancer and after years of a good fight to live, he died leaving a young family alone and in the wilderness of grief. How does a family carry on?
- A teenager went into seizures and after arriving at the hospital, his parents were told their son was dead. How does an empty and broken heart find comfort?
- A college student died in a fraternity house fire. How do friends, girlfriend, and family heal through devastation?
- A forty-six-year-old father with small children was heading home after a professional football game. He experienced chest pain and stopped at a convenience store for help. There he died of a massive heart attack. Where does a family gather courage to go on?
- A best friend's father committed suicide. How do we live with tragic unanswerable questions?
- A colleague at work lost a baby. It was full term and stillborn. What can we say to help?
- A friend's child was born with a physical and mental handicap. How do we sojourn with him or her in the years ahead?
- An employee was suddenly laid off at work and devastated. Then she found out the company went under and all her retirement savings were lost. How do we pick up the pieces when everything is lost?
- A college senior, dreaming of the day he would marry his fiancé, suddenly was crushed because she ended the relationship. How does one survive loss and rejection at the sametime?
- A hospital nurse was recently diagnosed with breast cancer. Now she is having difficulty concentrating on patients' needs. How do we calm our fears and anxiety?

Yes, all of us have been or will be touched by loss and grief. Many have asked and yearned for the answers to difficult questions. "How do I get through this?" And many have asked, "How can I help my friend, spouse, or co-worker get through this?" This is what this book is about.

So many well-meaning friends and loved ones may try to cheer us up rather than just be with us in our sadness. Rather than help us grieve through and talk out our pain, they may attempt to talk us out of pain. Rather than be sojourners with us in the wilderness, they may attempt to find us a shortcut. Although they love us deeply, they may not understand that the grief wilderness takes time and the roads can have hairpin curves. They may not understand that we need to feel through, think through, and talk through our dark grief in order to find the light again.

This book is not designed to take you out of your pain but to invite you into and through your pain to transformation and new life. It is not written to give you the perfect thing to say to make another feel better, but to help you listen and sojourn with others in their pain.

Although written for the person in the wilderness of grief, this work is also for professionals, laypersons, and friends who want to be better sojourners. This includes the minister, priest, rabbi, spiritual director, counselor, therapist, teacher, grief coach, nurse, physician, and other health care professional, as well as, caring family member, friend, and neighbor. If you are a leader of people or an executive, the people you lead will at times go through difficult losses. This book will guide you in effectively supporting them through tough times.

Throughout history, clergy, nurses, physicians, and ministers have observed human loss and grief. Professionals from most fields of behavioral science, pastoral care, and medicine have continued to extensively research and write about the subject. The distinction of *The Unwanted Gift of Grief* is that it integrates the behavioral sciences with theology, spirituality, and religion. Through my eyes and ears as a hospital chaplain and a professional therapist, the reader will be taken to the bedside, emergency room, trauma center, and therapy room. Real dramas and grief stories will bring to life the meaning of the wilderness of grief. As the reader, you are invited into these intimate and tragic experiences. The names have been changed, and in some cases details altered, to enhance privacy and anonymity.

For more than thirty years as a hospital chaplain with Memorial Hermann Healthcare System, and as an individual, marriage, and family therapist, I have been privileged to sojourn with many fellow strugglers. They have taught me much about grief and suffering. They have taught me the aged old truth that it rains on the just and the unjust. They have taught me the miracle and courage of living through and after a loss.

In the confines of these pages, I will not address every type of loss. The list is endless. However, I have included many. You will read about the losses of infants, children, spouses, colleagues, and friends. You will read about tragic accidents, trauma, terminal illness, dying, and suicide. You will read of families who courageously carry on with mentally and physically challenged and sometimes ill children. These tender and sacred situations will be the stories used to illustrate the spiritual walk through the unwanted gift of grief.

You likely will not identify with many situations described in the pages ahead. Also, these stories may be more dramatic than your story. I encourage you to take whatever insight or encouragement you can from these situations and apply them to your particular loss and healing process. We all grieve differently, perceive loss differently, and are helped differently.

Grief is similar to a roller coaster ride. It has its profound dips. The more we talk together before the roller coaster ride, the less anxiety and panic we feel when we get on the roller coaster. At the amusement park, we talk about it before we get on its extreme highs and sudden drops. We talk and scream while on the ride. Then we process our relief and experience after the ride.

Grief is like that ride on the roller coaster, except that grief's ride will not be ending soon. Talking before we get on the roller coaster of grief may reassure us that we are not going crazy when grief does hit. We just feel crazy! Crying, mourning, and perhaps screaming on the roller coaster of grief, may help us cope with its sudden dips and turns. Talking about our feelings and thoughts after a tragic event may help us regain equilibrium and peace.

The chapters ahead are an invitation for you to enter the wilderness of grief and not avoid it. In one of the greatest sermons in history, Jesus preached on a mountainside a sermon called the "Sermon on the Mount." This sermon included the famous Beatitudes. One of the Beatitudes states, "Blessed are those who mourn, for they shall be comforted" (Matthew 5:4 RSV). We are invited to mourn. Comfort comes to those who mourn. This does not say that those who finish their mourning will be comforted, or those who avoid mourning will be comforted. This says that those who mourn will be comforted. Mourning itself is comforting and leads to healing.

Throughout the pages ahead you will read of my Christian faith perspective. Without this faith my pathways may not have traveled toward the light. However, this book is intended for all of God's people, whatever your faith, spirituality, religion, belief, or unbelief. We all have losses. We all grieve. I hope this book will speak to those of every faith perspective.

OVERVIEW OF THE BOOK

Part I clarifies the meaning of the unwanted gift of grief and my belief that grief is gratitude. It invites the reader to enter and grow through the wilderness of grief, rather than resist it. This section will include factors that affect our grief work and the importance of realizing that everyone grieves differently.

Part II clarifies common human experiences in the grief wilderness. Real people are the teachers. Names have been changed in order to protect their privacy. Perhaps by understanding the losses, suffering, and healing stories of others, you will find hope and, if you are a sojourner, you will become more skillful in facilitating hope.

Part III offers specific guidelines and suggestions for sojourning with others. Taken from years of chaplaincy ministry and teaching in one of the largest hospital systems in America, these guidelines are designed to enhance your ability to help others heal. A sojourner is one who is willing to support, listen, and compassionately walk with another through their wilderness of grief. This section clarifies the empathy, the self-emptying nature, specific skills, and knowledge needed to significantly sojourn with another. It offers detailed steps the sojourner and the grieving person may want to take in crossing the wilderness together.

Part IV includes a brief section on the effects of grief on marriage and family. Marriage is tough enough without loss and grief. Possible differences in the way women and men grieve are explored as a way of defining the "distance escalating cycle" that can take place in some intimate relationships during the grief wilderness. This distancing cycle can add to misunderstandings that are already common between two intimates facing loss and grief together. This is especially true after a loss of a child or a prolonged illness of a child.

The effects of grief on sexuality and sexual closeness are explored. A guide is included for helping couples mourn together on grief dates and make it through the wilderness together. These guidelines can also be used by family members or in relationships where both persons are going through losses simultaneously.

The last chapter includes fifty ways for making it through the wilderness of grief. These suggestions are from individuals who have been through it. Perhaps some of these suggestions will help you. Not all of these ideas are helpful to every grieving person. We are all helped differently, just as we all grieve differently.

Often when we are in the throes of grief we have difficulty concentrating or reading for long periods of time. Because of this, I have offered text boxes on many pages to help you focus on brief ideas in the event you cannot concentrate on the entire text.

Remember, I am inviting you into and through your grief and pain, rather than away from it. Using the unwanted gift of grief is the "way" to emotional and spiritual growth and profound transformation and healing. If at all possible, find a sojourner to walk with you through this wilderness.

PART I:
THE UNWANTED GIFT

Chapter 1

Grief As Gratitude, Grief As Gift

THE WILDERNESS OF GRIEF: THE "WAY" TO TRANSFORMATION

Many words and pictures come to mind when I think of the journey through grief, but I keep coming back to the word "wilderness." The wilderness is not just a physical place but also a spiritual and emotional place. In the wilderness of grief we may not know which direction to take. Feelings of fear may paralyze us. We may not be able to see through the thick forest to tomorrow. Our courage may fail. In the wilderness the body, mind, and spirit journey through dry deserts, blinding rains, lonely storms, long nights, and dormant winters—searching for springtime. We search for light and hope and have no assurance that the direction we travel will lead to either. We wait for morning while stuck in mourning. We hope we are mourning toward morning. When I use the word "wilderness," I am describing a "way" rather than a physical place. The grief wilderness is the "way" of the journey toward healing and a promised life again.

The wilderness of grief is not just a physical place but also a spiritual and emotional place. The wilderness is the "way" of the journey toward healing and a promised life again.

Grief As Gratitude

This book was not written to make you feel good. Reading this statement must seem strange given that this book is designed to at-

The Unwanted Gift of Grief: A Ministry Approach
© 2006 by The Haworth Press, Inc. All rights reserved.
doi:10.1300/5644_02

tract readers who are in the midst of grief and those who minister and care for those grieving. Although this book is not offered to make you feel good, it is offered to help you feel what you feel and hopefully better understand what you feel so that you will go into and through the wilderness of grief toward better healing.

Grief as gratitude may sound crazy, but don't put this book down yet. Give me a chance to clarify myself. I believe that grief is often the expression of our gratitude. Grief is a painful adjustment period after any significant loss. It affects our body, mind, emotions, and spirit. We go through this painful adjustment period because we have lost a significant person with whom we had a meaningful and treasured relationship.

Grief is a painful adjustment experience after any significant loss engaging our body, mind, emotions, and spirit.

We only grieve profoundly for those with whom we have had a relationship and close connection. We may be momentarily sad and sympathetic regarding another person's loss, a friend's divorce, a tragic suicide, a schoolyard shooting, or a terrorist attack taking many lives. For a while we may be struck with identification, sorrow, compassion, and empathy for them. However, we only experience ongoing and high volumes of grief, pain, and confusion when we have had significant involvement with the deceased person. Unless a person was close to us, we tend not to grieve at length and depth.

Usually we only experience high volumes of grief when we have had a significant involvement with the person who is no longer with us. Unless a person was close to us, we tend not to grieve at length and depth.

We only grieve profoundly for those with whom we have had a significant relationship and close bond. We treasure them and are grateful for their closeness in our lives. This gratitude is the source of our pain. When we express grief for them, we are expressing gratitude for them. The pain, anger, and sadness are our expressions of gratitude for them.

After a loss, our hearts may feel broken or throats may tighten with emotions. Our tears may flow or leak uncontrollably. Our thoughts and emotions may collide in confusion, anger, and frustration. Sadness and depression may pull us into a pit. We experience this because the person was important to us and we love him or her. These grief experiences are expressing gratitude to God and life for that special one.

I do not mean that we are grateful for the loss. On the contrary, we hate and mourn the fact that our loved one is not here with us. Nor do I mean that we should be grateful for the pain. On the contrary, with all our might we want the pain to lift. Nor do I mean that this is God's will, so therefore be grateful. No! This is not what I mean when I say grief is gratitude!

What I mean is that our emotions, groaning, angry laments, broken heart, and emptiness are expressions of our gratitude and praise to God for the person who is no longer with us. After a loss, we may cry out in anger or frustration toward God and life. Even this is an expression of gratitude. After a loss we may plunge into dark sadness or depression. This also is an expression of gratitude. So do not let anyone hurry you through your tears and grief. Don't let anyone try to take away your grief until you are ready.

When we express grief for our loved one, we are expressing gratitude for him or her.

Grief Is Unwanted

No one wants to live with physical or emotional pain. After a significant loss we go through an unwanted wilderness of both. After the loss of a baby, it is difficult to be with friends who have babies or to attend a best friend's baby shower. Sometimes we avoid them or find an excuse not to attend. After the birth of my daughter, Abby, it was difficult to be with friends whose babies were developing normally. The grief was great.

After the death of a spouse, it is painful to go to bed alone at night. The bed is empty and tears may become our only companion. Some sleep at a friend's house for a while to help cradle the grief and loneliness. No one wants the grief wilderness, yet, it seems that the mourning process is universal and common to all. Although everyone experiences and expresses it differently, sooner or later we all tell the story of unwanted grief.

No one wants the grief wilderness, yet it seems that the mourning process is universal and common to all.

Grief Is a Gift

Grief is a gift is a concept that is difficult to believe and accept, yet grief has many important functions and outcomes. Grief fills up the vacuum of empty space left by our deceased love one until we can adjust to and accept the reality that the person is no longer with us. It is a gift that facilitates our separation and differentiation from a lost love and heals us toward a new future. But this gift takes time and hard grief work.

Grief fills up the vacuum of empty space left by the deceased until we can adjust to and accept the reality that the person is no longer with us.

Grief is an adjustment period after any loss and involves painful work of the mind, body, emotions, and spirit. This is often called grief work. This means that a significant loss throws us into disturbing thoughts in our minds, disturbing physical changes in our bodies, disturbing feelings in our emotions, and disturbing spiritual wondering and wandering of our hearts and souls. These painful disturbances of grief are the gifts that thrust us into labor and contractions and give birth toward new life after loss. For example, disbelief and shock may be helpful spiritual shock absorbers keeping us on the road of life until we can find our way. Frustration and anger can be the vehicles for standing up again and refusing to be a victim. Releasing frustration can help us work through our inability to control life. Sadness and depression can be ways of connecting with our deceased love, until we can let go and live life to the fullest again.

The painful disturbances of grief are the unwanted gifts that thrust us into labor and contractions that birth new life after loss.

Our Creator has given us these gifts of grief in order for us to manage the loss of love on earth. Love is a powerful gift. It takes time and work to create love and it takes time and work to adjust to its loss.

Many types of loss and feared loss can bring on this wilderness of grief: death of a spouse, family member, or friend; loss of health; terminal illness; birth of a child with a mental or physical challenge; divorce; job loss; geographic move; child with a severe or terminal illness; end of a love relationship; loss of a pet; and many more.

Love is a powerful gift. It takes time and work to create love and it takes time and work to adjust to its loss.

Although we do not want to experience the wilderness, it is an important sojourn toward healing, new life, and a deeper self. You may want to avoid the wilderness, but the fastest way and the most effective way is through the wilderness. Not wanting to experience grief, we often try to avoid it by going around, over, or under it. But the way is *through.* Perhaps you have heard it said, "If you don't grieve your grief, your grief will grieve you." It is true. The body has its way of acting out in illness and behavior what we do not attend to in the grief process. By going through grief we develop the spiritual muscle and the inner resources that lead to wholeness and health.

We may want to avoid the wilderness of grief, but the fastest way and the most effective way is through the wilderness.

When we fall in love with someone, it can be a slow bonding or a love-at-first-sight experience. Either way, we continue developing the bond gradually through time and togetherness. We negotiate needs and, at times, hurt and disappoint each other. Energy is given to putting our lives together in terms of roles, goals, love, sexuality, finances, family, and future. It does not happen all at once, even when we are in a hurry. Romantic feelings of well-being and being loved are tremendous, but take time to wed together. Songs, poems, and books are written about these love stories.

This energy power of love also creates the undertow of grief after the loss of a loved one. Songs, poems, and books are also written about these losses. Spend some time listening to country music or the blues and notice the lamenting. The unbonding of love can be just as powerful a gift as bonding. Unbonding is the part of loving and losing that we hate. It takes a wilderness of time, separation anxiety, and renegotiating life before we can let go and say "yes" to life again and move on. After such loss we must slowly renegotiate our roles, goals, love, sexuality, finances, family, future, etc. In many ways the music of lost love is about utilizing the gift of grief in order to productively mourn and adjust.

The power of love also creates the undertow of grief after the loss of a loved one.

Everyone Grieves Differently

You may not agree or identify with everything I write in the pages ahead. The reason is that we all grieve differently. Our personalities, perceptions, worldviews, losses, relationships, family histories, cultural influences, and spiritual beliefs are all different. All of these affect the way we grieve.

WITHOUT FACING THE PAIN, GROWTH MAY BE LIMITED

Throughout the life cycle we have had to die in order to live. The new baby grieves leaving the perfect, warm, calm womb of the mother and must labor through the birth canal and adjust to the cold and lights. The infant must adjust to an imperfect world. Going off to school for the first time can be a powerful loss. The child leaves the security of home and family and may experience grief in letting go of babyhood and taking on childhood. Growth brings with it emotional and spiritual growing pains. The child must grieve through the way life had been and adjust to the new way of the classroom. If the child is overprotected from this grief and adjustment, growth may be interrupted and inner emotional muscle and spiritual muscle may not develop as well.

Growth brings with it emotional and spiritual growing pains.

The same is true for the transition between the teen years and adulthood, young adult and mid-life, or mid-life and old age. Every step of life's growth also invites us to let go of the past, and usually brings a particular level of grief. These are often called growing pains. In this growth process there is much to grieve and much to gain. We can gain more courage, autonomy, and differentiation. This process of holding on to and letting go of, which is at the heart of healthy human development and love, is also at the heart of grieving. In other words, grieving is at the core of life development and growth. Letting go of the past, in order to grow into the future, includes pain, adjustment, and hard work. Grief work is the unwanted gift, but it is a gift.

The process of holding on to and letting go of, which is at the heart of human development and love, is also at the heart of grieving.

LETTING GO OF THE PAST,
WE RISE TO NEW LIFE

Only as one lets go of the past, can one find new life. The past is often that which we cherished, loved, and gave us meaning. We fear the new for now the future looks bleak, filled with unknowns and loneliness. This transformation process can be profound and is an experience no one wants.

We will not need to let go of that which we hold on to and enter the mystery of the unknown. We must enter the mystery with faith. The grief wilderness is the vehicle, the pathway, and "the way" through this transformation and resurrection journey. Faith is the fuel that feeds our spirit and courage as we cross the wilderness.

The grief wilderness is the vehicle, the pathway, and "the way" through this transformation and resurrection journey. Faith is the fuel that feeds our spirit and courage as we cross the wilderness.

The gift of grief is the process of transformation from the penultimate (that which one knows and experiences in the flesh) to the ultimate (that which is of mystery, God, spirituality, and not limited to the flesh). If we are willing to say yes to the pain and walk into the unknown, this transformation may lead to God, who is creator, sustainer, comforter, and redeemer of both the kingdom of love on earth and the eternal kingdom. This sojourn will transform us into a deeper and wiser person and toward a fulfilling life again. However, it is painful and earthy in spite of all the previous hopeful and positive words. If you are in the grief wilderness now, you may be saying, "Hogwash, Tim, it hurts too much!" The truth that life will never be the same is difficult to face.

If we are willing to say yes to the pain and walk into the unknown, transformation will happen. We will find God, who is creator, sustainer, comforter, and redeemer of both the kingdom of love on earth and the eternal kingdom.

The gift of grief is the process of transforming toward differentiation. Differentiation means to be different from another, yet connected in relationship to them. This is the process of growing up and maturing. As small children we were not differentiated from our parents. We were dependent and it was necessary to connect with them in order to be safe and loved. Growing up included the process of differentiating from parents, while taking their love with us and within us and continuing on to create autonomous and unique lives as adults.

When we lose a love in death or in divorce, we enter a similar process of differentiation. We go on to find our autonomous identity without the other being physically with us. While differentiating from him or her, the hope is that we internalize the person's love for us and create a new life. We let go, move on, and live more fully and lovingly because he or she loved us. We internalize the memories and take them with us into love and life, rather than letting these memories bind us in mourning and solitude for the rest of our lives.

We internalize the memories of our loved one and take them with us into future love and life, rather than letting these memories of them bind us in mourning and solitude for the rest of our lives.

The last gift you give your lost love is not your grief, although it is a gift and true tribute to him or her. The last and most lasting gift and tribute you give is creating a new life and going on to live fully because that person loved you and you loved him or her. This is the transformed differentiated heart.

GRIEF: A JOURNEY OF WONDERING
AND WANDERING IN THE WILDERNESS

After a significant loss, we enter a wilderness of disturbed thoughts, feelings, behaviors, and spirit. Often one wonders, "This isn't like me!" This is often followed by, "What's wrong with me? When will I be normal again? How will I make it?" We may wander around going every direction and yet not know for sure which direction is the right direction. When we get to a destination on the journey, we do not want to be there. The intensity and duration of the grief is usually in proportion to the meaning, bond, and intensity of the relationship with the deceased loved one. The wilderness of grief and adjustment usually goes on for months and even years. For some who refuse to enter the wilderness and refuse to do grief work, it can have a paralyzing effect for a lifetime.

The intensity and duration of grief is usually in proportion to the meaning, bond, and intensity of the relationship with the deceased or lost loved one.

One may roam aimlessly for a while wandering and wondering around for new direction, hope, and happiness. God may be experienced as absent or far away. Similar to the children of Israel searching for the Promised Land, our soul searches for a promised life. We search for eternal and human comfort from the storms, droughts, and hungers that besiege the human spirit in grief. We search in every direction: North, South, East, and West. We often yearn for God and wonder why He is silent. At times, we search for anyone who will comfort us. In this wilderness we often have faith struggles as we vacillate between faith and doubt, hope and despair, and courage and fear.

We often wonder why God is silent. In the wilderness, we often have faith struggles as we vacillate between faith and doubt, hope and despair, and courage and fear.

Over the months and years of grief, change, and transformation, we discover that the promised life is not somewhere out there in a distance, such as, in a new place, in a new love, or in a new baby. We discover that the promised life is the differentiated heart and soul within us. There we find peace, hope, and new meaning. But first we wrestle in the wilderness with the unwanted gift of grief.

Chapter 2

Everyone Grieves Differently

There are no authorities when it comes to grief. This is the first principle I try to teach and live by in my counseling. I am not an authority. Many professionals similar to myself work with grieving people and study or write about grief, but we are not authorities. We are observers. When it comes to grief, the authority is the person grieving. No one can predict how you will grieve or how long you will grieve. However, professionals and spiritual leaders of every age and culture have closely observed persons in grief and have experienced grief themselves. From these observations and experiences, we have written stories and findings and drawn conclusions.

When it comes to grief, the authority is the person grieving.

Even though many ministers, psychologists, social workers, physicians, and other professionals have observed and identified a common grieving process that may unfold with some similarities in phases and stages, not everyone needs to nor will experience grief this way. The same is true about what you read in this book. Although I identify common threads I have observed in grief, you may not and need not experience them. Everyone grieves differently! You will journey through grief your particular way.

You will journey through grief your particular way.

The Unwanted Gift of Grief: A Ministry Approach
© 2006 by The Haworth Press, Inc. All rights reserved.
doi:10.1300/5644_03

When people talk about their grief, I am amazed at the connections and identifications they make with one another. More amazing is the fact that each person tells a different story of grief even when her or his loss is quite similar. Even though two persons may have experienced the same loss, each interprets and experiences it differently. This is the reason it is not usually helpful to say, "I understand what you mean; I have been there." The following are just some of the ways we do grieving differently and why we do it differently.

HOW LONG WILL I GRIEVE?

We have often heard that time is the great healer. I don't believe that. Yes, time does help us put grief away, get some distance, and go on. But time is not the great healer. What we do with time is the great healer.

Time is not the great healer. What we do with time is the great healer.

When I speak at conferences, seminars, and support groups, I am often asked, "How long will this pain go on?" I get a little anxious about responding to this question because people in the group have had different experiences. At times, they express how angry they feel toward professionals who lay out a universal time frame in which all persons should adjust successfully through grief. Although they may not want to hear any predicted time frame, for some reason they continue to ask.

My response to the question is that grief is so personal and particular to each loss and each person that the length of an adjustment and healing time cannot be predicted. Let me share some comments made by those who have been through grief and some of my general conclusions.

Grief is so personal and particular to each loss and each person that the length of adjustment and healing time cannot be predicted.

Most say that there was something astonishingly different after a full year of seasons. It seemed to relate to going through all the firsts—the first holidays, birthdays, death anniversaries, and other anniversaries. They found each season also had its memories to grieve. Memories such as family snow skiing in the winter, working in the yard together in the spring, barbecues in the summer, kids off to school in the fall, Christmas, Hanukkah, Thanksgiving, birthdays, and others. Every family has rituals for each event and the first year seems to hit hard as they face these traditions and memories.

Many report significant healing movement after the first year. However, others say the hardest time was the second year. After the shock and pain of the first year, their friends moved on and expected them to move on. These individuals suddenly realized in the second year that "this is forever, it's not going away." Some reported more aloneness and loneliness in the second year.

Families find that each season of the first year has memories to grieve.

Certainly the first year is traumatic and one wrestles with significant changes. As I listen to others, the following is my best fact-gathering response to the question of "How long?" Moving to an acceptance of one's loss may take from one to two years. Full transformation and healing may take up to seven years. Even after these years, one does not want to forget. On birthdays and holidays we may regrieve or replay the loss in mind and spirit, then pick up and move on again.

Moving to an acceptance of one's loss may take from one to two years. Full transformation and healing may take from up to seven years.

Frequently the next question is, "Does that mean I should not be involved with someone or get married again for seven years?" or "Should I not try to have another baby before I am over the death of my deceased child?" The answer to these important questions is whether you are trying to replace the person or child you lost with your new love. Love your new love or child for who they are as unique persons. We need to talk about and explore these issues as we begin life anew.

Many who fall in love or remarry are still working on the healing process. We need to be open about where we are in the healing process with those whom we date or establish new relationships with.

Decisions made prior to healing have their risks, yet the relationship may be an important part of the continued healing process. But if you chose remarriage, enjoy it. If you chose another pregnancy, enjoy it. Remember that love is never limited. Love makes more room in the heart, not less. Don't let your worry about grieving perfectly make new love more complex and risky. However, when you are still in considerable grief and starting to date, I encourage you to slow down and enjoy dating before limiting and focusing on commitment.

Remember that love is never limited. Love makes more room in the heart, not less.

THE EFFECTS OF FAMILY AND CULTURE ON GRIEVING

The way we grieve has much to do with what I call family and cultural language. We learned verbal and nonverbal messages about grief from our family, parents, and culture prior to ten years of age. These early experiences are recorded in the brain, and are usually unconscious and create automatic or involuntary behaviors and attitudes. These behaviors are often based on learned beliefs.

In seminars, I frequently ask a participant to tell the rest of the group how to use a fork without showing us how to use a fork. Some people are better at this than others, but most seem to stammer and struggle to describe how to use a dinner fork even though they could show us very quickly. Picking up the fork and using it is easy, but to explain without demonstrating is difficult. The act of eating with a fork is unconscious to us. Through repetition we internalize how to use a fork without thinking consciously.

The ways of grieving that are involuntary or unconscious to us are what I call family and cultural language. Family language is that which we repeatedly observed or experienced in the family. Cultural language is that which we repeatedly observed or experienced in our culture, ethnicity, or religion over many years of childhood. These events and messages become internalized to the point that we do not think about what we do, we just do it automatically and often unconsciously.

Then I ask the seminar members to tell me what their family, religion, and culture taught them about grieving. Hopefully, they can remember experiences before ten years of age. How did their family members grieve? Did they talk about it openly or remain in silence? Did they cry or become stoic? Did they avoid the grief and emotional pain? Did they just stay busy?

When I ask these questions, I get a wide range of responses, such as: "I can't remember that far back" or "I remember when my grandfather died or my mother died." We tend to grieve the way we were taught by family, gender, and cultural models before ten years of age. Please notice the word "tend." This is not true for everyone, but most everyone.

We tend to grieve the way we were taught by family, gender, and cultural models before ten years of age.

If no one in your family cried openly when your father died, you may have internalized messages not to express your grief openly. You may go on automatic unexpressive pilot when someone you love dies. You may find yourself crying quietly and alone. Or you may feel ashamed or inadequate about your grief because it was not openly permitted or modeled. On the other hand, if your family cried openly and talked through the emotional pain together, then you probably learned that it was acceptable to cry and talk openly about it.

Our gender models from our family also affect our grieving. If in the midst of loss the men in your family left the room and did not talk about grief or shed a tear, your family language may have taught you that men do not grieve openly. These models may have unconsciously taught you that men are to be stoic, distant, and tough. Usually these decisions about how to grieve are not made consciously. We just go into our feelings, thoughts, and behaviors as an unconscious reaction.

All of us have gender expectations based on our family and cultural history. For example, based on our gender role models there are certain ways that we expect women and men to act. If this is not brought into our conscious awareness, we may either repeat the past without thinking or develop a reaction formation.

A reaction formation may be when we make conscious or unconscious vows not to be like mother, father, or other family members. This can cause us to go to the opposite extremes. If your mother grieved on and on and it frightened or embarrassed you, then as an adult your grieving may have developed a reaction formation. You may have become unexpressive and stoic.

If your family talked about death and the loss openly, then you will probably talk openly as an adult. If your family withdrew in busy-work and avoided the expression of pain, you may find you have a propensity to stay busy and not express the pain, even to the point of becoming a workaholic. This becomes a way of avoiding emotional pain and grief.

Obviously, we each have different family language and cultural training and this can create conflicts in close relationships (e.g., marriage). We may have different needs in the midst of grief. For example, one spouse may need to cry and talk about the death of his or her daughter, and the other spouse may need to avoid the tears and conversation. This can create a collision of needs. These differences, although quite normal, may create distance and isolation from the one we love the most. Marriage is tough enough without the wilderness of grief.

We each have different models and family language for grief. This can create conflicts and misunderstanding in relationships because each individual may have different needs in the midst of grief.

Family and cultural influences often teach us how to or how not to grieve. Every family is different. Every culture grieves differently.[1] The more we consciously choose how to manage and grieve through the wilderness, the healthier we become in our healing process.

DIFFERENT PATHWAYS THROUGH GRIEF: THINK PEOPLE, FEEL PEOPLE, AND ACT PEOPLE

I continue to experience and identify different types of people amidst grief. These people relate differently to the world, friends, and family. Each perceives and struggles through grief differently.

The Think People

Think people use the cognitive pathway. They live, love, and grieve primarily from the cognitive pathways of the brain. When they grieve, their language is typically filled with facts, analyses, logic, linear thinking patterns, rationality, and reasoning. They are dominantly analytical in nature. In grief these people may share facts about what happened but tend not to share feelings. They may analyze what is happening but not emote. They may "think through" what is happening in the tragedy, but may not be able to "feel through." Their emotional expression may be flat as they relate the details of the tragedy. This may be learned as a small child from family language and may also be a genetic propensity. The response of others about this person may range from, "Isn't he handling his daughter's death well?" to "I can't believe he has no feelings about his daughter's death!"

The "think" people tend to use the cognitive pathway through grief.

The Feel People

Feel people tend to use the pathway of emotions. They live, love, and grieve primarily from the emotional pathways of the brain. When these persons grieve, their language is usually filled with emotive words such as happy, sad, angry, hurt, or fear. They tend to cry openly and express feelings. They think in circular patterns and may not always communicate with exact logic. They may "feel through" what is happening in the tragedy but may not be able to reason or "think through" what is happening. They may emote but not be able to think straight or keep thoughts organized. This also may be learned in early development and may have a genetic source. The response of others around this person may range from, "He is falling apart. He will never make it through this." to "I am so glad he can cry it out, it will help him get through this."

The "feel" people tend to use the pathway of emotions through grief.

The Act People

Act people may use the pathway of actions and behaviors. They may live, love, and grieve primarily through behaviors and actions. The people around them may not know what act people think or feel. They just see them in behaviors of action or inaction. These persons act out their feelings. They may sit in frozen silence unexpressive to all around them, put a hole through the wall with their fist, or throw things. These people tend to stay busy doing tasks during grief. They may get busy with funeral arrangements, cooking, or mowing the lawn. For months after a trauma or loss, they may work longer hours and not be able to sit still. The more they grieve the busier they may be. They tend to not talk about their feelings or name their thoughts. Often when asked by others about their thoughts and emotions, they may not be able to name them. They may explode or implode and the people around them may not understand their behavior. The response of others may range from "He has his work, he will make it through this loss." to "He is going to explode if he doesn't talk to someone about this loss."

The "act" people tend to use the pathway of actions and activities through grief.

The act people can be more difficult to understand, so let me illustrate. After her stillborn infant was delivered, I went by to visit Alicia in the hospital. She shared openly her tears and thoughts as she told me the story of her child. His name was Joshua. She already had Joshua's room decorated. This was her first child. I listened as she cried and talked. She was obviously a "feel person" with a fairly strong capacity to be a "think person" as well.

I asked how her husband was handling the loss of Joshua. She responded that she was not sure because he had left the hospital soon after delivery and gone home. She said that her husband, Gerald, was at home making a coffin for Joshua and that this was the way he worked through his feelings—by using his hands to make the coffin. She said it was difficult for him to talk about Joshua or cry openly with her. He did not know what to say to her when she cried. Gerald was an "act person" and Alicia was correct in her understanding of his way of grieving. Everyone grieves her or his own way. The problem was that Alicia could easily become isolated while not being free to share her grief openly with Gerald because of his busyness. Gerald may withdraw because he is uncomfortable with Alicia's emotions. Over time they could possibly become isolated from each other.

You may be asking what is the best way to get through the grief wilderness. What type of person handles this best? Is it best to think through? Feel through? Act through? Actually each of these people have their strengths and weaknesses in regard to going through the wilderness. My suggestion and encouragement is that we develop all of these capacities in our grief work and our everyday lives. Each of us has been given the capacity to think, feel, and act, even though we all have a propensity for what we do most of all, second of all, and third of all. The healthiest grieving process is when we can think through, feel through, and take action through our grief.

We need to develop all of these capacities and use all the pathways through grief. The healthiest grieving process is when we can think through, feel through, and take action through our grief.

Our differences may also become a problem. If we have a tendency to use only one of these pathways through the wilderness, we may not be transformed as completely as we hoped. Because of our tendencies, it is often easy to misunderstand one another. Alicia may need her husband's presence in order to share her tears. She may try to understand his way but may slowly feel lonely and abandoned. If after the funeral Gerald stays busy as a way to cope with his grief, Alicia may begin to feel hurt, distant, and angry toward him for abandoning her. Gerald, on the other hand, may feel misunderstood because Alicia does not realize the depth of his pain. If after awhile she withdraws in hurt and anger toward him, then he starts feeling unloved. Love for him means doing things or being busy together. He may conclude that Alicia is not getting on with life because she continues to cry and needs to continue talking about Joshua. The more she expresses her emotions the more helpless and anxious he feels. So he stays busy.

We must develop and use all the parts of ourselves. We tend to marry our opposites and use their strengths to complement our weaknesses and vice-versa. Yet, our spouse is also our teacher. Our spouse can, if we allow him or her, teach us how to get through the wilderness using all of these God-given resources. Our *thinking* can lead us to new ways of feeling and acting. Our *feelings* can lead us to new ways of thinking and acting. Our *actions* can lead us to new ways of feeling and thinking. All are important. All are gifts to be used.

Our thinking *can lead us to new ways of feeling and acting. Our* feelings *can lead us to new ways of thinking and acting. Our* actions *can lead us to new ways of feeling and thinking. All are gifts to be used in the wilderness of grief.*

Strengths and Weaknesses

The following are a few of the strengths and weaknesses of each of these types of people as they go through the wilderness. These are not offered as a way of labeling people. I hope these can help you understand yourself and the loved ones around you.

Strengths of the Think People

- May more readily take negative thoughts and re-frame them into positive thoughts
- May more readily read a self-help book and find that its concepts are helpful
- May think more clearly, even in the midst of crises and grief

Weaknesses of the Think People

- May express emotional pain through cognitive worry, pessimism, and/or obsessive thinking
- May often become debative and argumentative as a way of expressing sadness, anger, or frustration
- May often repress and suppress emotions that may later come out in other unhelpful ways

Strengths of the Feel People

- May more readily cry it out or anger it out and, as a result, feel better
- May more readily regress to the inner child's feeling level and grow up again emotionally
- Letting out emotions may release emotions that can, otherwise, negatively affect physical health

Weaknesses of the Feel People

- May fall into a deep pit of emotions and not be able to think clearly
- May experience deeper levels of depression and sadness and not be able to function
- May not be able to benefit as readily from a self-help book

Strengths of the Act People

- May go into action during the immediate crisis and this helps them cope with the loss
- May retreat into "busywork" and hobbies and this helps them get through
- May more readily release emotions and grief through physical exercise

Weaknesses of the Act People

- May become workaholics or "busyholics" to avoid grief
- May be misunderstood by others because they can not as readily talk about grief or express emotions
- May explode or implode and others may not understand why

As you read this, try to identify your personality characteristics and those of the one you love. Remember the goal is to use all of the pathways in the grief wilderness.

INTROVERTS AND EXTROVERTS

Other personality characteristics also affect the way we do grief. Introverts tend to get energy from going into themselves. They heal from the inside out and benefit from times of reflection alone. Introverts may often be silent and say little about the thoughts or pain within, while they go into their internal sanctuary for healing. Persons around them may not understand what they are experiencing and, thus, may not ask in order to support them. Often, the introvert needs this distance in order to grieve, recoup, reenergize, and heal, but sometimes this can lead to isolation.

Introverts may often be silent and say little about the thoughts or pain within, while they go into their internal sanctuary for healing.

On the other hand, extroverts tend to gain energy by being with others. They may heal from the outside in and benefit by being with others and talking, sharing, listening, and crying with them. They are healing within but it is as they process pain into words and experiences with others that their emotions lift. Extroverts need human closeness in order to grieve, recoup, reenergize, and heal, but sometimes are unable to handle solitude.

Extroverts may often gain energy and healing by being with, talking with, and crying with others. They usually need human interaction in order to grieve and heal.

Children in the same family are different. One child may need to talk and cry in the midst of grief, while another may need to be silent and ponder. One child may want to be in interaction with family members, while the other may go off to a bedroom to process the loss and pain. The difficult challenge for families in the grief process is reading each person's needs and responding with mutuality and empathy.

The difficult challenge for families in the grief process is reading each person's needs and responding with mutuality and empathy.

We need to become more balanced. We need to develop our introvert self and our extrovert self so that we use all our resources in the wilderness. This is especially important in intimate relationships where both have different needs. In these intimate relationships, we at times need to empty out of our personality preferences in order to meet the other's needs, as well as our own. We need to meet in the middle to help each other grieve.

Chapter 3

Factors That Affect the Wilderness of Grief

Many factors affect the intensity of grief and the way we grieve. Not only do people grieve differently but circumstances also affect the intensity of the wilderness. The meaning of the loss, the depth of the relationship with the deceased person, life cycle needs, involvement with people who love us, sojourners who walk with us, and more affect the way we grieve. This chapter addresses some of the factors that affect the journey through the wilderness of grief.

THE FAITH FACTOR

Faith is the spiritual fuel that sustains and guides us through grief. This faith factor enables us to transform and transcend life and death. However, in times of grief we often may experience God as far away, silent, and not caring. In the midst of pain, it is natural to become angry with God or filled with questions for Him. We may feel that we often receive only silence in return. Some conclude that there is no God or this tragedy could not and would not have happened. We may even search for God's unseen jaw and want to take a swing in frustration. This is normal and acceptable and God will receive our pounding fist and return our fist to us with mercy.

Faith is the spiritual fuel that sustains us and guides us through grief. This faith factor enables us to transform and transcend life and death. However, in times of grief we often may experience God as far away, silent, or not caring.

The Unwanted Gift of Grief: A Ministry Approach
© 2006 by The Haworth Press, Inc. All rights reserved.
doi:10.1300/5644_04

This spiritual wrestle is important. We do not ask questions of one in whom we do not believe is "there." We do not get angry and frustrated with God unless we believe that God "is." We do not say to God, "Where are you, God?" unless there is a deep profound belief that God is mysteriously a part of our life and pain.

People in pain often describe feelings of isolation, loneliness, and the silence of God. "Why can't God take the pain away? Why does God allow this to happen? Where is God? Why is my child dead? Why not take me instead?" When persons express these wrestling prayers and questions, they often feel they are in a monolog. These laments and experiences are a natural part of the journey in the wilderness and dialog with God.

Throughout this book I will address the faith factor. But don't expect the answers to easily satisfy you. The broken heart and hurting soul cannot be easily satisfied with quick answers.

The broken heart and hurting soul cannot be easily satisfied with quick answers.

Let me make a few comments about the faith factor. I do not believe God causes tragedy to happen for some mysterious purpose hidden up His sleeve. I am not comforted when people say, "Just remember, this is God's will or God has a reason." Although this may lead to a vigorous discussion regarding the various theories of God's will and the meaning of evil and suffering, in the midst of intense grief these theories can seem empty emotionally and spiritually. The academics of this discussion often are of disinterest to the one in intense grief. When someone has loved and lost and is told that it is God's will, this seems to speak of a God who is selfish and cruel.

I am not comforted when persons say, "Remember, God has a reason for this."

I do not believe God causes our losses for his purposes, but I do believe that God will be with us to find healing and purpose out of our losses and struggles. I do not believe God *took* your loved one but I believe that God *received* your loved one.[1] Your loved one was and is carved in the palm of God's hand. I believe God weeps with us in our pain and losses.

I do not believe God causes our losses for a purpose, but I do believe that God will be with us to find healing and purpose out of our losses and struggles. I believe God weeps with us in our pain and losses.

Keep wrestling with God. Keep asking the unanswerable questions. These questions help us engage the meaning of mystery. We will discover that when we face mystery, we may not ever know the answer, but we may come to live more faithfully in mystery without the answers. The questions we ask are part of the way that we creatures come to accept the unbelievable. Beware of people that give you quick and easy answers in order to make you feel better. *Inspirational repressive faith* can postpone the gift of grief and may contribute to illness. Inspirational repressive faith is when our faith and beliefs inspire us to suppress and repress the emotional pain and lament we feel in the midst of suffering. This may not be helpful or healthy.

Repressive faith may sound similar to the following: "Don't cry. Don't mourn. God is with you. Don't express your anger at God. Be grateful and do not question God's will. Only if you have faith without doubt can the miracle of healing take place. Just remember, God has a reason." These well-meaning people and statements can often cause us to bury our grief, rather than express it openly and honestly so that our soul can empty it and release it. People with suppressive and repressive faith may become dishonest with their emotions and spiritual struggle, while trying to look faithful for God and others. God already knows our heart.

Repressive faith is when we use our beliefs and faith to suppress and repress the emotional pain and lament we feel in the midst of suffering and grief. This type of faith can delay healing.

Inspirational expressive faith is a faith and belief system that inspires us and encourages us to express our grief openly, honestly, and sometimes angrily, in order to release the human pain that binds us. This faith knows that because God cares and loves us, we can express our lament and soul's anguish to God and others. These emotions are God's gifts to us and are vehicles to be used to transform us toward healing and toward the future. This faith says, "My God! My God! Why hast thou forsaken me?" We may need to join Job, the Psalmist, and Jesus in the deserts of life or in the Garden of Gethsemane. There we may lament and release the pain in our hearts and souls. God can handle this and invites us to place our heavy burden and groaning upon Him. We may not know how to pray, but the Spirit of God translates our groaning into words that are understandable to God (Romans 8:26-27, RSV, interpretation mine). When we express our suffering we heal more wholly and "holy."

God knows our hurt, pain, sadness, and anger already, so why not tell Him the truth? The gift of grief is given to help us heal. We do this through open and honest expressions of grief, lament, and prayer. Remember, our grief is our gratitude to God for the love that we have experienced with another, not gratitude for the grief and loss. So be grateful and grieve openly with your God.

Inspirational expressive faith is a faith and belief that inspires us and encourages us to express our grief openly, honestly, and sometimes angrily in order to release the pain that binds us. This faith helps us heal.

At the conclusion of a grief seminar, a young mother told me her story. Her son, Jason, had a birth defect that always leads to death before puberty. Through tears, she shared with me the bottom line that Jason was six and slowly dying. But that is not what she came to tell me. She went on to say that she had always been very religious but lately felt angry with God. She could not pray and had difficulty going to church. She also felt guilty about her feelings of anger toward God. She had stopped praying for Jason's healing because she was trying to accept the fact that he was going to die. When this mother talked with her pastor about her anger, he responded by telling her she needed to stop being angry with God. He told her to get her soul right with the Lord, and that God could not heal Jason if she remained angry.

As I listened I found myself disappointed with this pastor and his limited view of grief and God's mercy and grace. This is what I remember saying to her. "I can understand why you are angry with God. God can understand it more than I. Have you told God openly and honestly how angry you are?" She just stared at me for a moment and said "No." I asked her to be open and honest in her groaning and prayers. "Tell God exactly how you feel. God can handle your anger, even though your well-meaning pastor cannot."

My comments of grace and permission led us into a long, tearful, and painful conversation in which her grief and anger poured out. Jason probably is dead by now. I hope she is still wrestling with God. We have to get close to God in order to wrestle with Him. I hope she is using the gift of grief and anger to get close to God.

We have to get close to God in order to wrestle with Him. Have you told God openly and honestly how angry and hurt you are? By doing this, you may be helping the healing process work and come to feel closer to God.

I hope God is a personal spiritual power in your life. We need this personal yet transcendent sojourner to wrestle with us in the wilderness, or stay awake with us during long nights. We need this personal and transcendent sojourner who mysteriously knows our human pain and cries with us. I hope when the bottom drops out of life, you will find that you are joined by the Holy Comforter, who cries with you and carries you. The faith factor dramatically affects the way we wonder and wander in the wilderness of grief.

I hope that when the bottom drops out of life, you will find that you are joined by the Holy Comforter, who cries with you and carries you. The faith factor affects the way we wonder and wander in the wilderness of grief.

THE NEED FOR SOJOURNERS: COUNSELORS, MINISTERS, AND FRIENDS

A sojourner is one who listens and encourages us to talk about the real pain and struggles in the wilderness. A sojourner may be an old friend, running buddy, pastor, counselor, health care professional, or a new friend. The real pain and struggles are often that which we don't share because people seem too busy, insensitive, or quick to give us advice and empty encouragement. Most of all, the sojourner is one who understands the process of grief at some basic level. His or her understanding of grief may come from studying, but usually comes from his or her own grief experiences. As the wounded heal through loss, they frequently take the next step in healing, which is to become a wounded healer for others.

A sojourner is one who listens and encourages us to talk about the real pain and struggles in the wilderness. The real pain and struggles are often that which we don't share because people seem too busy, insensitive, or quick to give us advice and empty encouragement.

The sojourner is not one who tells us his or her story or tells us what to do. On the contrary, he or she is able to listen, support, and help us tell our stories in the wilderness. If he or she does all the talking or has only advice to give, find another person to be your sojourner. If you and your sojourner are both in grief, which is not unusual, take turns listening. More detailed characteristics and guidelines for sojourners are found in the chapters on sojourning. Ask your sojourner to read this book. This will give you each an understanding of your relationship and the sojourner's objectives.

As the wounded heal through loss, they frequently take the next step in healing, which is to become a wounded healer for others.

A sojourner may meet us over coffee at our place or their's, or at a church office, or in a private corner of a quiet restaurant. I suggest some place where you can cry and not keep up a public facade. It's great if you play together, i.e., shop, play cards, golf, at times, but have specific times set up just for grieving and talking about your loss. At first, you may get together every week for an agreed-upon length of time. As the wilderness moves toward healing, you may want to meet every two weeks, then three, once a month, and then just as needed. You may need to meet more frequently at first when the burden is heavy.

Does this sound similar to therapy? Yes, we may make a therapist/counselor/pastor our sojourner, but the sojourner does not have to be a professional. This is not therapy, although it may be therapeutic. Our sojourner needs to be someone we trust with our pain and story and be an active listener. Many times this may not be our best friend or spouse. Not because we don't trust him or her, but unfortunately we often edit our pain and story in order to protect our close loved ones. The sojourner needs to be one who is there for us and can hear the depth of our soul.

Our sojourner needs to be someone we trust with our pain and story and be an active listener.

Professional Counselors, Clergy, Physicians, and Other Ministers

Professionals can certainly be our sojourners. But even if you choose a nonprofessional sojourner, you may also need to work with a professionally trained physician, pastor, or therapist in order to get help, coaching, and insight in the wilderness. Be sure that these professionals are well trained in the area of grief. When depression hits harder than usual, grief brings up issues and anxieties from the past, we have difficulty functioning, or when sleeping and eating are disturbed for long periods of time, we may find it helpful to work with a professional.

Ask around for someone in the community who specializes in grief. Try to find someone who respects and can work with your spiritual issues. Usually you can get a name from a local pastor, priest, rabbi, hospital chaplain, or local support groups. If we are blocked in the wilderness, counseling may help us unblock and move on our way toward healing.

If we are blocked in the wilderness, counseling may help us to unblock and move on our way toward healing.

SUDDEN LOSS OR SLOW, UNFOLDING LOSS

Whether we lose someone suddenly or slowly over months and years of illness, both can affect differently the way we grieve. If our loved one had been sick for a long time prior to death, we may have done a great deal of grief work and adjustment prior to death. Day by day and teaspoonful by teaspoonful, we may have started the journey toward healing before our loved one died. This does not mean that a volume of tears and grief did not come at the time of death, but it may mean we had already been doing anticipatory grief work. Sometimes we experience relief along with profound grief at the moment of death. We may feel relief that our child no longer suffers. We may feel relief because our spouse was so discontented in a nursing home.

If death and loss come suddenly, the wilderness can start like an unexpected earthquake to the soul. The tremors of grief can shake the ground of our being for months and years. In sudden loss, the grief is compressed in time rather than slowly unfolding. In slow losses we often have an opportunity to say good-bye, whereas in sudden loss we were left with good-byes unexpressed and relational business unfinished.

In sudden loss, the grief is compressed in time rather than unfold slowly. In slow losses we often have an opportunity to say good-bye. In sudden loss, we are often left with good-byes unexpressed and relational business unfinished. In slow losses we grieve a teaspoon at a time.

REJECTION AND SUICIDE

Some losses involve a greater sense of rejection than others. These may be divorce, suicide, job layoff, death of a parent at a young age, or death of a person with whom we were in unresolved conflict. I am sure you could list others. In most of these situations there are feelings of rejection and abandonment, which can compound pain. These feelings and thoughts of rejection and abandonment can wound the self and our self-esteem.

After death we tend to glorify the lost one and glorify the relationship we had with him or her. In divorce, suicide, and some other losses, we often feel a sense of failure and guilt. Not only do we feel rejected, but also we may feel "rejectable." Not only do we feel unaccepted, but also we may feel unacceptable. These losses can lead to intense depression, anger, or guilt. Many times we do not want to share with others because the loss seems either unacceptable in society's eyes or we fear rejection. The family whose child or family member dies of AIDS-related causes often experiences this. The family whose loved one commits suicide also can experience this. Any of these may cause complications in adjustment and healing.

Experiences of rejection may cause complications in adjustment and healing after a loss. Not only do we feel rejected by someone but also we may feel rejectable.

Most survivors of loss feel a sense of abandonment in normal grief adjustment, but they usually know that even in the midst of their pain they were loved. However, some may feel that God has rejected or abandoned them. Their questions and lamentations may express this. These feelings and thoughts may complicate the grieving process and may need special attention.

Suicide

Facing life after a loved one commits suicide is a devastating challenge. Not only may this wilderness involve a sense of shame about what our loved one has done, but a sense of rejection, guilt, and anger. Our shame is usually focused on society's view and moral teachings that life is sacred and we should care for and value our lives—mind, body, and spirit. Because some may believe our loved one broke this value, the family can unfortunately experience so much shame that they withdraw into a lonely vacuum. Rather than talk about the tragedy of suicide and the profound grief that comes with it, they may hibernate.

Friends may withdraw because they do not know what to say or fear they will embarrass the family if they bring it up. Suicide is truly a disenfranchised loss and grief. Members of the organization Survivors of Suicide (SOS) know how disenfranchised their loss and grief can be.

After a suicide, the ones closest to the deceased often experience guilt because they believe they should have noticed a problem and done something to prevent it. Survivors may replay what they consider as mistakes that occurred in the months leading up to the person's death. The depression may have been evident and family may feel guilt or regret because they did not make the person get help. In some cases the family has supported, encouraged, begged, and even demanded the loved one get help and he or she did not. Still the guilt can flow because they failed to succeed in these efforts. Children often conclude that they cause things to happen and may take responsibility for this suicide as well. Children need close love, observation, and repeated assurance after a parent, sibling, or friend commits suicide.

Also, the family may experience anger and frustration toward the one who took his or her life. Perhaps they are angry because the deceased gave up or angry because he or she did not get help, or angry because their loved one did not value life. Perhaps they are angry that the deceased did not love his or her children or spouse enough to think about their feelings and lives after the suicide. At times the anger is with the health care professionals who may have treated this loved one, but did not succeed. Or the anger may be with close friends who do not understand clinical depression and the suffering that the disease can cause.

In many situations, loved ones feel guilty for feeling so angry with the one who committed suicide. Caught between their feelings of anger and feelings of guilt, they may experience depression beyond the expected sadness that comes after a tragic loss. Not being able to be openly angry or express their guilt feelings binds them up more. The anger also may turn inward on the self in the form of guilt.

In most cases suicide is the result of a chronic ongoing illness called clinical depression. Or it may be the result of depressed feelings and thinking in reaction to a severe loss or problem in recent months. For example, one can become depressed after the loss of a spouse. But in most cases it is the result of a chronic disease such as clinical depression, bipolar personality disorder, or an acute loss with severe adjustment disorder to the loss. In this depression the individual sees no hope or future.

In my language let me describe the complicated "lifeview" of many who are clinically depressed or at risk of suicide. The chemicals in the brain cause the computer of the brain to misfire. Rather than thinking logically and hopefully, our thoughts become illogical and hopeless. The brain's neurotransmitters misfire for short or long periods of time. The individual feels so down, sad, despairing, pessimistic, hopeless, helpless, worthless, inadequate, empty or more, that he or she becomes focused on how to get out of the hopeless situation and the emotional pain. Irrationally, he or she concludes that the only way to relief is death. Frequently the individual irrationally concludes that his or her spouse, children, or others will be better off without him or her. In this irrational state, the person may convince himself or herself that his or her death would be a better way of loving them than to be alive. This state of being and thinking is so sad to observe and must have professional medical care. We now have many medical resources for treating depression.

If a person is clinically depressed, get him or her medical care. A well-intentioned lecture, sermon, shaming, or pep talk usually does nothing to help this person. These efforts may only reinforce feelings of being worthless, hopeless, inadequate, and better off dead. If you know someone in this state, get him or her help. But remember, you cannot control the outcome. Even with significant support, some depressed individuals who are getting professional help may still commit suicide. This disease is a difficult challenge for everyone involved.

We all have days of hopelessness and loss of future, but this is not the disease I am speaking of here. Any time we begin to have sustained suicidal thoughts or want to hurt ourselves, we need to see a physician, counselor, health care professional, or turn to a clinically trained clergy. Get help! But in order to be helped, we must be honest about what we are thinking and feeling. There is hope, but right now we may not see it. We need professional help until the clouds and storm of depression lift and we can see light and hope again. Hope will come, if we stay in the pain and get help with it.

People often feel embarrassed to admit that they are on an antidepressant medication. If our thyroid is not producing, we welcome medication and talk about it. If we have severe high blood pressure, we welcome the medication and talk about it. But if our brain chemistry is not working correctly, we often shy away from medication and are afraid to talk about it. When will we fully and appropriately use God's gift of medicine?

Family members often ask how God sees and responds to suicide. "Is my husband in heaven?" may be one of the ways the question is focused. The ultimate answer to this belongs to God. However, I can tell you how I, in my limited understanding, understand God and what I think some of the answers are to these questions.

God understands our diseases with greater wisdom than we do. God understands that we are people with weaknesses and strengths. God understands our failures and brokenness, compassionately graces our depression, and forgives suicide more profoundly than we forgive each other and ourselves.

When we measure a person's goodness, one must look beyond his or her disease. We must look to his or her whole life, not just focus on the depressed episodes or illness. We need to look to whether he or she loved God and others, not just look to those final moments of despair when he or she in an irrational state could not love himself or herself. We need to look at what he or she believed and "faithed" in over a lifetime. This tells us more about the person's eternal condition than a tragic temporal human mistake on earth.

Please understand something else I believe. God calls us to ideal! God's ideal for us is to love and enjoy God, our neighbor, and ourselves all the days of our lives, just as God loves and enjoys us. To commit suicide is not the ideal of God. But we must remember that God meets us in the "real," in the throes of our lives and, at times, at our worst. God's love for us is not based on our perfection or obtained ideal but on the fact that we are all God's children. God meets us where we are and calls us to grow toward Him. When depression leads to suicide, I believe that God meets us in our real pain and failures, hurts with us, and mercifully receives and forgives us. When it comes to suffering, clinical depression and suicide, I believe that God knows the heart and soul beyond our human brokenness.

In a counseling session, I listened while a widow talked about her husband's death. He had committed suicide a few months before. The grief, rejection, guilt, shame, and anger had been powerful emotions throughout our work together. On this particular day, she was talking about her love, acceptance, and forgiveness of her husband. This was not cheap grace. She was still angry and deeply disappointed that he took his life, but her words were moving toward mercy and forgiveness. She clarified that she knew her husband loved her and that she wanted to forgive him. On some days she completely forgave him, but on others she could not. She discussed his suffering and depression. Although she did not understand his suicide, she was moving to a place of reconciliation, mercy, and forgiveness. If she could forgive, how much more God loves and forgives.

Our Involvement in the Relationship

The intensity of the wilderness is usually in proportion to our involvement in the relationship with the deceased person. Years ago when my father called to tell me that my aunt had died, I thought about her for an hour or so. I was sad for a while, but I was perhaps more sad for my Dad because he lost a sister. I had not seen my aunt very often since early childhood. She lived in another state. Because money was tight, we seldom made the trip to her home. Our mobile society can have this effect on family relationships. The distance can mean we have little close feelings for them.

The intensity of the wilderness is usually in proportion to our involvement in the relationship with the deceased person.

On the other hand, when my mother died the experience was altogether different. Mom died while she and I were in the middle of a conversation. I was stunned, shaken, saddened, and lost. I felt this not just for an hour, but also for months and years. At times I reflected on her life, death, and contributions to my life. She gave me unconditional love. Mom and I had involvement and bond. Mom mattered to me. My volume of grief for my mother was in relationship to my gratitude for her and my involvement with her.

THE LIFE CYCLE AND DEVELOPMENT

Our age and developmental stage can have a profound effect on the intensity of grief and the way we grieve. My mother died when I was forty. I was a grown man with my own family and could provide for myself emotionally and physically. But what if I had been two, five, or perhaps thirteen? Each age and developmental stage in life has its own needs and neediness, as well as, insight and wisdom.[2] These affect the journey through the wilderness. The more autonomous and differentiated we are in our development and personal identity, the more internal resources we have for crossing the wilderness of grief.

Each age and developmental stage in life has its own needs and neediness, as well as, insight and wisdom, which affect the journey through the wilderness.

What if you are in your mid-twenties and have two small children? You have been raising your children and not working outside the home for several years. Your husband is killed and you have little insurance coverage. The grief would be powerful enough in losing a love, but add to that the loss of income and care for the children. This can add many levels of anxieties and complications to grief.

What if you are in your early twenties, a college junior, and feel you have life by the tail, and then suddenly the woman you loved for three years and planned to marry ends the relationship? Add to this young man's loss another factor. His mother died when he was four years old. His grief can be severe and complicated. Losing the girlfriend is painful enough, but the grief is compounded by the loss of mother in early childhood. A loss in childhood can easily include feelings of abandonment. The loss to this college student may not only stir up abandonment issues in the present, but also stir up abandonment issues from the past. This may cause profound grief and depression.

The life cycle, with its wisdom and painful past, can have a profound effect on grief. The public or friends may not understand the depth of an individual's loss and the developmental history the person brings to that loss. For that matter, the person grieving may not understand it either. The past can have disguised effect on grief in the present. This is why it is so important to allow the individual who is grieving to tell us his or her story rather assuming we understand.

Our past can have profound and disguised effects on grief in the present.

DIFFERENTIATION AND ENMESHMENT

Throughout this book I make reference to the task of differentiation in the grief process. What is differentiation? Differentiation is not only a big word but also a lifelong task. Differentiation is the capacity to be closely connected with another person, yet still have our own separate identity. On the other hand, the enmeshed person may have the ability to be closely connected with another person, but does not have a separate identity. Children in early stages of life are not separate in their identity from the parent and naturally not differentiated. This is why a loss to a small child can be devastating, especially if the loss is a parent.

Differentiation is the capacity to be closely connected with another person, yet still have our own separate identity.

One of the lessons we must learn in this life is to be *in* the world but not *of* the world. This means to be connected with others but not worship or have all our identity wrapped up in them. In life and in marriage, we develop close relationships and together we structure our lives, family, and love. When we lose someone to death, part of our identity is lost and must be reshaped over a long period of healing and transformation. We have to differentiate from that loved person and the life we had together in order to heal and go on with our lives. We do this by internalizing this person's love and taking that love with us as we recreate a new life. If while in the relationship, we did not have separate identities, interests, friends, and activities, the differentiation work in the grief wilderness may be much more complex.

One of the lessons we must learn in this life is to be in *the world but not* of *the world. This means to be connected with others but not worship or have all our identity wrapped up in them.*

One of the goals of healthy wholeness is interdependence. Interdependence is when we have healthy need for each other but not neediness. Let me explain. We all are an empty bucket needing to be filled with the water of love from others. But we all have holes in the bottom of our buckets, so that the love we receive drips out and we return to each other for more love to fill our buckets. Some of us have holes in the bottom of our buckets that are much too big. These people need too much love. This is emotional dependency. On the other hand, some do not recognize their own need for love and become so independent that they isolate and lose connection with others. They become sealed-off buckets and sealed-off people. This is counterdependency, the opposite extreme of dependency. We often call this independence, but indeed it is not. It is a form of dependency.

When we lose someone, part of our identity is lost momentarily and must be reshaped over a long period of healing and transformation. We must differentiate from that loved person and internalize his or her love and take the love with us as we recreate a new life and new love.

One of the objectives of living is to develop healthy and relaxed interdependency. If our bucket has too many emotional holes, our challenge is to go down into the deep waters of our lives and see why and what needs to be done to close up some of the holes. Then love can sustain us longer.

During the wilderness of grief our needs for love are usually stronger than in everyday life. This is partly because we lost our human source of consistent love.

During the wilderness of grief, our need for love is usually stronger than in everyday life. The emotionally dependent person needs too much love and care. The emotionally independent person may avoid people and become isolated. Both factors can negatively affect healing. We need others, yet we need to make it through the wilderness to new identity and autonomy. We loved our deceased spouse, yet we must differentiate from our spouse in order to go on and walk with God into new life as a separate and single pilgrim.

Grief causes us to go back and work with our emotional development and issues of neediness. We often regress into feelings of the inner child of our past. All of us carry the inner child of the past with us in our grown-up adult bodies. A loss, tragedy, or crisis can throw us back into childlike feelings and issues from the past so that we must rework some of the issues from the past, while grieving a loss in the present. Our need for support from friends, family, sojourners, and professionals is very important as we heal and grow up into adult interdependence again.

A loss, tragedy, and/or crisis can throw us back into childlike feelings and issues from the past so that we must rework some of the issues from the past, while grieving a loss in the present.

The Value of Support

The way we manage through the wilderness is dramatically affected by whether we have emotional and spiritual support. Many support people can be found on the journey. Family, friends, community, faith group, sojourners, support groups, professionals, and running buddies are all important on the long journey. Without their support the process of adjustment and healing is more difficult. These persons may become God's incarnate care in the wilderness.

Many kinds of support people can be found on the journey. These persons may become God's incarnate care in the wilderness.

The church or congregation includes people who can walk with us. In the beginning, it may be difficult to go to congregational activities because this may be a place that brings memories of our loved one and the activities we shared with him or her. Perhaps it is difficult because well-meaning folks say silly things to us, hoping to make us feel better. In spite of all this, the community of faith can be of tremendous support. But, it takes courage to go. Yes, it takes courage.

Support groups are very important. I encourage clients to attend support groups at least four times, because they usually spend the first few sessions resisting being there. They too quickly decide they do not like the group prior to giving the group a chance. Just being there can bring back pain, and some want to avoid it. There are effective and ineffective support groups. So if one doesn't fit you, find another. But give it a try for a few meetings before you draw your conclusion.

I encourage clients to attend support groups at least four times because they usually spend the first few sessions resisting being there. Just being there can bring back remembered pain and it is so natural to want to avoid pain.

When Joan lost a sixteen-year-old daughter, she attended the Compassionate Friends support group. This is a national organization with chapters around the country for parents who have lost a child. Joan not only found support, but she made some lifelong friendships. She not only participated but also became a facilitator and a regional leader. For years, she created support networks for people all over the nation and became a personal sojourner to many.

During Compassionate Friends meetings, professionals are invited to speak, but plenty of time is allowed for sharing and grieving among new members and veterans. There are moments of suggestions, but most of the conversations are about support. A box of tissues is always being passed around. In this community you can discover you are not alone, although everyone present has a different story. They begin each session by introducing themselves and their deceased child and how their child died. Having a place to share their child, to remember and cry seems to have an energizing effect on these parents. If a member does not want to talk or can't, one can just say "I pass."

Another type of support group is Life After Loss, created and sponsored by the American Cancer Society. This group is for those who have lost a loved one to death, usually in the past three years. The group is unique in that it has a time limit and is not ongoing as with many support groups. Usually led by health care professionals and clergy, each of the six two-hour sessions has a specific curriculum related to moving through grief. Time is also allowed for sharing and support. This group is one of the finest I have been associated with.

Support groups, if organized well, can have the power to facilitate change and healing. Support groups are all different. Some are educational and others are just support and sharing stories. Some groups are facilitated well; some may not be as effective. When Abby was born, we attended Parents of Children with Down Syndrome. This was a powerful experience of support, education, and fun. Many of these parents have remained friends for a lifetime.

We need friends. Don't drop out of the weekly bridge group, although for a while you may be so preoccupied and depressed you may lose every game. We need friends to shop with, talk with, walk with, play with, and cry with. Soon we become aware of which friends we can do grief work with and which ones cannot handle our grief. Don't retire them as friends, but don't stop looking for a sojourner who can listen to the real stuff of your grief.

We need friends to shop with, talk with, walk with, play with, and cry with. Soon we become aware of which friends we can do grief work with and which ones cannot handle our grief.

We need to play and have fun. But if that is all friends are doing for us and all we are doing for ourselves, there may be some avoiding of grief going on. Have fun, but watch your diet of fun. Keep it balanced between play and grief work. Often if we don't enter the wilderness and do the work of grief, our grief can get stuck and take longer to work through. I recommend a grief sojourner.

Everyone grieves differently, and different factors affect the way we grieve in the wilderness. We need to be aware and sensitive to these factors.

PART II:
THE WILDERNESS OF GRIEF

Chapter 4

Unbelievable Darkness

The wilderness of grief often begins with darkness. This darkness can last for moments, days, weeks, or months. Whether this darkness hits after the news of a terminal diagnosis or the birth of a child with retardation or whether it hits in the middle of divorce, job loss, sudden death, or loss of a baby, the darkness and disbelief can hover over us like an unexpected tornado. The darkness is often experienced as shock, feeling faint, or a profound sense of denial, which comes with the difficulty of facing the unbelievable. We want to push the truth away and deny the reality of what has just happened.

The darkness is often experienced as shock, feeling faint, or a profound sense of denial, which comes with the difficulty of facing the unbelievable.

THE DYNAMICS OF DARKNESS

One of the first experiences of the wilderness is shock, confusion, and disbelief. Our mind and emotions cannot accept or believe the traumatic news we have just heard or experienced. We may experience visual darkness or changes in vision. This cloud of darkness may hover over the human spirit and soul and momentarily shuts out the painful reality. We just don't believe it. It just cannot be true.

Our mind and emotions cannot accept or believe the traumatic news we have just heard or experienced. We may experience visual darkness or a darkness in our spirit and soul.

The Unwanted Gift of Grief: A Ministry Approach
© 2006 by The Haworth Press, Inc. All rights reserved.
doi:10.1300/5644_05

The gift of this shock, darkness, and denial is that it gives the person time to prepare for the truth and the long journey into the wilderness toward acceptance. For awhile its function is to push away reality until the self and soul can face reality. It helps us take the trauma a painful teaspoonful at a time rather than drink the whole cup at once. In hospital ministry and my counseling practice, I have witnessed various types of darkness and shock.

Darkness and Disbelief

Typically we experience some darkness and disbelief after encountering the tragic. It may be experienced as numbness, lightheadedness, confusion, mentally avoiding the present, forgetfulness, and more. This can range from mild shock to pronounced faintness. These dynamics are an attempt to distance or disassociate the self from the tragedy. If we can disassociate ourselves, than we may try to convince ourselves it did not happen in the first place. We often say things such as, "I can't believe this! No, that isn't possible! But I just talked to him!" or just "No! No! No!"

The gift of this shock, darkness, and denial is that it gives the person time to prepare for the truth and the journey into the wilderness. For awhile its function is to push away reality until the self and soul can face reality.

The disbelief is often accompanied by changes in blood pressure, heart rate, and auditory or visual perception. The person may feel faint, clammy, or dizzy and may forget things such as everyday telephone numbers. Obviously this is not a time to drive an automobile or make major decisions. This is also a time in which we need trusted and supportive friends around us.

TYPES OF SHOCK AND DISBELIEF

"Life As Always" Shock

This form of shock or denial takes place when the individual, after being told of a loss or serious health problem, may move into a state of "life as always." We may carry on as if nothing has happened or perhaps vow to ourselves, "I am just not going to get upset about this!" Emotions may be trapped or repressed within. The body or facial expressions may show little or no emotional affect or change. Grief is absent. Others often interpret the absence of grief as, "Isn't she doing well, or isn't she handling the situation well."

The body or facial expressions may show little or no emotional affect or change. Grief is absent.

This state can go on for hours, days, or even months as we push away the pain by convincing ourselves that the event did not happen or that we will not let it get us down. This may lead to a physical illness or emotional depression. If we do not use the gift of grief, express it, and enter the wilderness of grief work, our grief may work its way out in other forms. We must heal from the inside out, not just on the outside. This later method may mean that pockets of pain never get dealt with while we are looking fine on the outside to others.

This state can go on for hours, days, weeks, or even months as we push away the pain by convincing ourselves that the event did not happen or that we will not let it get us down.

I was paged to the intensive care unit (ICU) early one morning. Elizabeth, a woman in her mid-fifties, had come in during the night with chest pain. The nurse paged me because the woman had been crying during the night but would not talk about her situation. The nurse thought perhaps the patient would talk to a chaplain.

We begin to talk, and Elizabeth slowly trusted me enough to share her story. Her husband had died five years before after a long battle with cancer. The volume and depth of her tears caused me to think that he had just died in recent weeks or months. I kept listening.

Elizabeth went on, "You see, Chaplain, when my husband was dying, he made me promise not to cry or be sad over his death. He asked me to always remember him and our time together with joy and happiness. Chaplain, until last night I kept that promise. I have kept that promise and have not shed a tear for five years. When I came in last night with chest pain, I could not hold back the tears any longer. I started crying and I haven't been able to stop." She continued to tell her story as tears rolled down her cheeks.

Then she said firmly and powerfully. "Chaplain, I think that is what broke my heart. That is the reason I have these chest pains. I can't tell you how good it feels just to cry and talk about him. I can see now I should have let these tears out a long time ago."

Elizabeth diagnosed herself. With further tests, doctors found no blockage to the heart, only change in its rhythms. Once the nurses and doctors understood the amount of grief and emotion she had bottled up in suppression and repression, they agreed with Elizabeth's self-diagnosis that the bottled-up unexpressed grief had changed the rhythms of her heart causing chest pain. Elizabeth was told she would recover and she was encouraged to keep grieving and talking it out.

In the next few days, I met with her often in order to help her mourn and catch up on her grief work. Grief is an unwanted gift, but a gift we must use. If we don't do our grief work, our grief may grieve us in some form of physical illness or symptoms.

If we do not do our grief work, our grief may grieve us in some form of physical illness or symptoms.

Computer Shock

Another reaction of darkness or disbelief is what I call "computer shock." In this shock, we push away the pain and the reality by moving into business as usual or into busy activities. It's as if we push a key on the computer and it prints a flurry of activities and directions that we must follow.

In this shock, we push away the pain and the reality by moving into business as usual or into busy activities.

Although the emotions are in us, we deny their expression and the activities become rituals that reinforce the suppression of grief. Often these persons are afraid that if they start crying, they won't be able to stop. The flurry of activity can be telephone calls, arranging the funeral, taking care of children, cleaning the house, working longer hours, exercising constantly, and more.

Mrs. Anderson appeared to be experiencing computer shock. She was called to the emergency room after her husband had been killed in a motor vehicle accident. She arrived at the hospital with two children who appeared to be young teenagers. They only knew that he had been in an accident.

Upon hearing the news, Mrs. Anderson went into action by immediately sending one son to one phone with instructions to call an aunt and two others. She sent the second son to another telephone with instructions to call an uncle. For the next two hours she stayed busy and she kept the children busy. She made more calls and planned the funeral and schedules at school and work. She stayed busy as if she had touched a computer key and it printed out her busy instructions. It concerned me that throughout this flurry of activity, she never expressed any emotional loss or sadness. The darkness came over her in the form of activities.

Everyone grieves differently. Mrs. Anderson had to grieve her way. But I wondered about the children. They were following her example. They stayed busy getting the jobs done with little expression of grief. I wondered to myself as they left the hospital: "Would the pain and emotions ever have permission to be expressed? What lessons were these two young men learning from their mother as to how to deal with grief? How long would this family avoid the open grief and tears in the future? If they continue this activity and deny grief its expression, how would the grief come out later?"

I had many concerns for them as they left the hospital, but I was also reminded that everyone grieves in his or her own way. Computer shock can last a few hours, days, weeks, months, years, or even a lifetime.

Computer shock can last a few hours, days, weeks, months, years, or even a lifetime.

Each family has its own ground rules and ways of grieving. The darkness of grief can fall heavy and cause us to push away all the pain with a flurry of activity. We may think that if we stay busy enough we will not have to enter the wilderness of grief.

Eruption-of-Emotions Shock

When darkness and tragedy strike, some go into immediate expression of strong emotions. In this form of shock and denial we may either move into an explosion or implosion of emotion. This may be falling to the floor wailing "No, No, No!," passing out, or going limp into withdrawal from reality. We may run out of the emergency room into the streets, hoping that in getting away this event will not be true. Perhaps by pounding walls with our fist or bashing our heads on the floor or wall, we are pushing against the envelop of reality. These strong reactions are a part of shock in the darkness of grief.

When darkness and tragedy strike, some go into immediate expression of strong emotions. In this form of shock and denial we may either move into an explosion or implosion of emotion.

Grieving persons can physically hurt themselves in the outburst of pain and shock. The caregiver needs to take action to protect them from the surroundings and sometimes from their own physical letting go. They may faint, or withdraw, as if, in an autistic state. The milder forms of this shock are seen in agitation or momentary withdrawal, sitting and staring, constant fidgeting, to walking or running, yelling, or in a barrage of words.

Hurting persons may faint or withdraw, as if, in an autistic state. The milder forms of this shock are seen in agitation or momentary withdrawal, sitting and staring, constant fidgeting, walking or running, yelling, or in a barrage of words.

I was called to the emergency room at 2:00 a.m. As I neared the family room I heard the wails of a young woman. But that is not all I heard. She was pounding her head on the floor with each wail of "No! No! No!" Occasionally she would call out her fiancé's name. She was covered with blood, but it was not coming from her body. The nurse and I forced a pillow between her head and the floor and let her scream. I could do nothing more, for she had verbally withdrawn from all of us into a volcanic eruption of grief. For awhile, all we could do was to protect her from hurting herself and let her do the dark painful work of grief.

A little later, I heard her story. She and her fiancé were at a night-club. They were backing out of a parking place and accidentally hit a man's pickup truck. In a fit of anger, the man in the pickup took out a shotgun and unloaded it into her boyfriend's face. Someone gathered him and the girlfriend into the back of a car and raced to the hospital while she cradled his wounded head. He was dead before arrival and she was in shock.

After an hour of crying out helplessly she went into an exhausted and limp state on the floor and seemed to sleep. A physician and nurse checked her vital signs frequently and treated her for shock. By 5:00 a.m. we were able to contact her parents. They were relieved that their daughter was not injured but distraught over their future son-in-law's lost life.

Finding courage to face reality, she came out of her sleep and slowly talked about what happened in the parking lot. She cried as she was told what she already knew in her heart: her future husband was dead.

It was a long dismal walk out to the hospital parking lot with the parents and young woman. The sun was beginning to rise. She did not notice that it was a beautiful morning. She probably would not recognize beautiful sunrises for a long while. The darkness of her grief had shut it out. I walked with the young woman as if she were my sister. She hardly knew my name, yet we deeply connected for those hours at a dark crossroads in her life.

TEMPORARY OR PERMANENT AMNESIA

Individuals may not remember the events of a trauma immediately afterward. Sometimes the memory is permanently unavailable to them. This is more common in trauma situations such as motor vehicle accidents, explosions, fires, rape, assault, childhood abuse, or other dramatic life-threatening situations. Often the amnesia is caused by physical injury, and yet it can be an emotional and cognitive response to a situation of fear.

Individuals may not remember the events of a trauma immediately after-
ward. Sometimes the memory is permanently unavailable to them.

When past trauma causes difficulties in living a normal life, it is often diagnosed as post-traumatic stress disorder (PTSD). Frequently as the person heals and feels more secure after the trauma or accident, the memories and the feelings associated with the trauma will surface into consciousness. This is the time in which we are saying to ourself, unconsciously, that we are strong enough to face this now. This can be hours, days, weeks, months, or later. However, the individual may never remember the specifics of the trauma. In some cases this may be a gift.

The amnesia may break through momentarily in the form of fear and anxi-
ety when we least expect it.

The amnesia may break through momentarily in the form of fear and anxiety when we least expect it. For example, after an automobile accident the fears and anxiety may return profoundly, as one rides in or drives an automobile. Certain sounds or expressed emotions can cause the anxiety to surface. Although anxiety or panic are experienced, the person may not make the connection between this present experience and the past trauma. During this time we need strong loving support and understanding. Frequently we need to talk and/or cry. We need help from sojourners to help us do this. The family may impatiently want their loved one to get on with life and put the trauma behind him or her, but the person may not be ready.

This is a time we need strong loving support and understanding. Frequently
we need to talk and/or cry. We need help from sojourners to help us do this.

Talking about these experiences and the thoughts, body reactions, and emotions that the experience engenders is an important part of working through the forgotten trauma and in coping with and managing these situations. At times more specific medical attention is needed with a counselor, clinically trained clergy, family physician, or psychiatrist.

At times more specific professional attention is needed with a counselor, clinically trained clergy, family physician, or psychiatrist.

Don't press yourself or the victim to remember the specifics that have been blocked out by this amnesia. If this is going to happen, it will surface and be remembered in its own time and when the person is ready. However, it is helpful to talk to trusted loved ones about the anxiety or fear when it surfaces. If our lives continue to be interrupted by past trauma, we may need support and help with professionals. One of the ways we deal with trauma is to express the emotions or remembered facts over and over, and also, to state over and over what we find to be unbelievable and unreal. This can lead to internalizing and accepting the experience and moving on with life again.

One of the ways we deal with trauma is to express the emotions or remembered facts over and over and also, to state over and over what we find to be unbelievable and unreal. This can lead to internalizing and accepting the experience and moving on with life again.

When trauma, loss, or the unbelievable happens, darkness may cover us. It's as if we cannot see the next step. We may need a patient and empathic listening ear as we express repeatedly the same messages of unbelief and darkness. With each expression, over and over, we may be coming to integrate this sad and tragic experience. Please, if you are the person in grief, share with someone you trust the many thoughts and feelings that ruminate around in your head. These vehicles of expression are gifts to be used for moving through shock and trauma. They will take you into the transforming wilderness of grief.

Chapter 5

Frustration and Anger Amid "Why?"

It was 2:00 a.m. and Abby had been born just a few hours before. She was our first child. I was impressed that the pediatrician came out in the middle of the night just to examine my baby daughter. After his lengthy stay in the newborn nursery, he suggested we go down to the doctor's lounge and talk. For the first time, I let myself realize *something was wrong—very wrong!*

As we sat down, the doctor spoke precisely and slowly. This was obviously difficult for him to explain to anyone and perhaps more difficult to clarify for a fellow hospital staff member. The conversation went something like this.

"Tim, I think we have a problem. I think your daughter has Down syndrome."

I didn't even hear it. Just the month before the nurse manager of labor and delivery asked me to do an in-service seminar for the nursing staff on how to help couples whose babies were born with retardation or deformities. One of the journal articles I read in preparation for the seminar had been about the grief of a young couple whose child was born with Down syndrome. In my shock and denial, I did not recognize what should have been a very familiar syndrome. I made the mistake of asking. "What does that mean, Doctor?"

Slowly and painfully he told me. "Down syndrome is a mental retardation that can be recognized by physical characteristics such as almond-shaped eyes, a smaller bridge on the nose, the tongue is usually larger than the mouth creating some difficulties in speech and . . ."

He went on as I entered a daze. He caught my attention again when he said, "Usually they can learn but these children are slower than others. These children have mental retardation and their intelligence level can range from the twenties up to the sixties or low seventies . . ."

The Unwanted Gift of Grief: A Ministry Approach
© 2006 by The Haworth Press, Inc. All rights reserved.
doi:10.1300/5644_06

He said more, but I could not focus any longer. I felt a little dizzy and faint. He offered his regrets, sympathies, and support, and returned to the nursery.

When he left, I was near a back hall of the hospital. I entered the private hall and cried and screamed, "Why? Why God?" I swung my arms angrily through the air wanting to land my fist on God's unseen jaw. "After all these years of waiting for a child until after seminary, taking my first full-time ministry appointment in this hospital and now you do this? . . . What have I done to deserve this? Where are you now, Lord?"

As I yelled out my lament to God, I was swinging my fist through the air. If people had seen me they would have thought I had gone mad. I am sure I looked like a two year old rather than a twenty-six-year-old pastor. In the Gethsemane of that lonely hallway, I felt totally abandoned. All I could feel was my brewing anger and hurt. "My God! My God! Why have you forsaken us?" Yet in yelling and releasing out the pain, another voice began to speak. This voice within was saying, "Tim, you can handle this. We will make this."

FRUSTRATION AND ANGER:
PART OF THE JOURNEY

Frustration and anger are siblings to the experience of grief. These feelings of lament and anguish are common and can help us move through the wilderness. As the anesthetic of shock and disbelief wear off, we often move into feelings of agitation, irritability, frustration, hostility, or raw anger. These feelings may be fed, like an underground spring, by the emotions of fear, helplessness, loneliness, sadness, and perhaps abandonment.

As the anesthetic of shock and disbelief wear off, we often move into feelings of agitation, irritability, frustration, hostility, or raw anger. These feelings may be fed, like an underground spring, by the emotions of fear, helplessness, loneliness, sadness, and perhaps abandonment.

Frequently these emotions are expressed by asking "Why?" If we are with someone who is asking the "why" questions, don't conclude too quickly that the person expressing this lament really wants an answer from us. In fact, there are no answers when it comes to the why of suffering. I have read numerous books on suffering and the will of God, and I still can't explain the why of our suffering. We may belittle them if in our response we try to give them an answer to the mystery of their loss. They may even be thinking, "Who has the audacity to think he or she has an answer? Who has the audacity to think he or she can explain the unexplainable?"

Frequently these emotions are expressed by asking "Why?" If we are with someone who is asking the "why" questions, don't conclude too quickly that the person expressing this lament really wants an answer from us.

The emotion of frustration and anger may be expressed in various ways: being short, critical, sarcastic, avoidant, impatient, throwing things, etc. Or frustration may be expressed in various forms of thinking: asking why, frustration with God, irritated with the world and the church, cursing the day we were born, and even holding ourselves responsible. These frustrations are the angst and anxiety humans experience because we are creatures and not Creator. In suffering, we as creatures discover that we can be in control of some things, but not everything. Frustration and anger can be strong when we find we cannot control loss or death. Frustration can be especially strong if we feel that God has abandoned us.

These frustrations are the angst and anxiety humans experience because we are creatures and not Creator. In suffering, we as creatures discover that we can be in control of some things, but not everything.

The positive strength or gift of frustration and anger is that it gives us a vehicle for releasing the pain and standing up with courage amidst mystery and tragedy. Rather than become victim to the tragedy, the anger may give us a temporary backbone, defense, and coping mechanism. People are often uncomfortable with lamenting frustration and anger and, as a result, tend to avoid expressing them. At times we even judge people who express anger. Frustration and anger are neutral emotions. In themselves, they are neither right nor wrong. The issue of right and wrong begins with what we do with our anger and how we express it.

The positive strength or gift of frustration and anger is that it gives us a vehicle for releasing the pain and standing up with courage amidst mystery and tragedy. Rather than become victim to the tragedy, the anger may give us a temporary backbone, defense, and coping mechanism.

The expression of frustration is different for everyone. For example, men tend to have difficulty expressing hurt, fear, and sadness, so they may express frustration and anger. Society has often taught men not to show hurt, sadness, or fear. As a result anger becomes an acceptable vehicle for expressing grief. We men have done some changing in recent years. We are beginning to learn to be more vulnerable with expressing the hurt, sad, and fear side of grief.

Women, on the other hand, tend to have more difficulty expressing frustration and anger. Women may feel more comfortable expressing grief's sadness, hurt, and fear. Society has often taught women not to express anger. As a result, for many women sadness and hurt become the acceptable vehicles for expressing grief. Women are also changing in recent years. I think they are learning to be more vulnerable with expressing directly the anger side of grief. Please note the word *tendencies.* Not every man or woman fits into these tendencies. Remember that everyone grieves differently.

FRUSTRATION AND ANGER AS REGRET, REMORSE, OR GUILT

Grief's anger and frustration take many directions and are expressed in many forms. The direction of anger that troubles me the most is when we direct our anger toward ourselves. Often we blame ourselves as we look for a reason for the loss. This can be expressed in terms of guilt, profound regret, or remorse. We search for ways that we could have prevented the loss or what we may have done to cause it. We may search for personal failure. "What did I do to cause my child to be retarded?" Another person might say after a husband's heart attack, "Why didn't I make him go to the doctor?" or "What sin have I committed? Why is God punishing me?"

Often in the grieving process we reflect on how we may have failed our loved one. Remorse and guilt may saturate our lives as, at times, we look back and remember how we may have made mistakes or failed our friend, spouse, or parent. We regret those situations when we were not our best or patient enough or loving enough with him or her. Now all the little things that may have bugged us about a loved one, seem so petty and unimportant. We wish we could turn back time and have the opportunity to love the person again and more perfectly.

Often in the grieving process we reflect on how we may have failed our loved one. Regret, remorse, and guilt may saturate our lives as we look back and remember times we have made mistakes or failed him or her.

In all our relationships, whether that be as friends, parents, marriage partners, we can easily go back in the past and count our mistakes. In grief the recognition of failure can at times seem overwhelming. Usually this regret, remorse, or guilt is enhanced by the finality of the lost opportunity to love and appreciate the person. It is also enhanced by the lost opportunity to go to him or her and resolve petty issues or conflicts.

In grief the recognition of failure can at times seem overwhelming. Usually this regret, remorse, or guilt is enhanced by the finality of the lost opportunity to love and appreciate the person.

These feelings are very real and normal in most grief experiences. This is especially true if we were in a conflict with the person just before death occurred. In relationships, we have all, at times, failed and come up short.

We may need resolution, reconciliation, and forgiveness with them and may, especially, need to forgive ourselves. This is dramatically true after a death. How can we internalize grace and forgiveness, when the one we may need it from is no longer with us on earth? These complex feelings and thoughts need a balm of forgiveness, acceptance, and grace that come from a merciful spiritual source beyond us. For me that source is our loving and forgiving God.

In relationships, we have all failed and come up short at times. How can we internalize grace, reconciliation and forgiveness when the one we may need it from is no longer with us on earth? These complex regrets need a balm of forgiveness, acceptance, and grace that come from a merciful spiritual Source beyond us.

Anger toward self can become an emotional and spiritual whip, which can contribute to depression, self-depreciation, and the feeling of being the guilty victim. Many people may curse the day they were born, as did Job. In this self-imposed whipping, we may be bordering on an attempt to be God. We may be trying to hold court in order to judge ourselves for causing the tragedy. Humans often carry the mistaken vision that we can control all things. We often carry the self-judgment that we could have changed this tragedy if only we. . . .

It is very common to blame ourselves as we look for a reason for our loss. We search for ways that we could have prevented this loss and what we may have done to cause it. We may search for personal failure.

At times we see God as the great puppeteer in the sky pulling the strings of life causing this tragedy because we have sinned or been inadequate. Thus, we think we brought this on ourselves. This can become a heavy load of guilt and lead to deeper depression and isolation from God and others.

The grief work we do with our sojourner can help us manage and work through this self-blame and regret. At first, it is quite natural to think of all our regrets and failures in relationship with the lost loved one, job, or marriage. We should understand these feelings of responsibility, but not condemn ourselves with them. All relationships of love have quarrels and make mistakes. But your mistakes did not purposefully make this tragedy happen.

The grief work we do can help us manage and work through this self-blame and regret.

FRUSTRATION AND ANGER TOWARD OTHERS

Toward the One Who Died

When left alone to pick up the pieces of life, we often become frustrated with the one who has died. When the surviving spouse or family member must learn the tasks normally handled by the deceased person, our frustration may surface. When income is cut in half or children must pick up more responsibility to complete the functions of the home, our irritation may simmer. Although the grieving person can yell or wail out the frustration at the departed person, the wailing often has no satisfaction or completion because the deceased loved one is not present in order to finish the quarrel with us. He or she is not physically present, so we cannot make up with him or her with a hug or kiss.

In a support group for widows and widowers, a seemingly frail senior citizen told her story. Some months after her husband died, she had a flat tire driving down a city street. She said she got out of her car, looked at the tire, and started kicking and cursing the tire. "I felt foolish, but it sure felt good," she said with a smile. And then she added, "It wasn't until I got home that I realized I wasn't mad at the flat tire, I was mad at Joe for dying. He always took care of our tires. I had no idea how to fix a flat; that was Joe's job." Then she laughed and cried at the same time.

Another moment of anger toward a deceased loved one went similar to this. When she arrived at the hospital, the medical staff explained to the petite woman and mother of teenagers that her husband had died of a massive heart attack. This was not easy but the physician clarified carefully and caringly. After awhile she asked if she could see his body. I asked if she wanted me to go with her. She was quick to say "yes."

When she stood viewing her husband's body, she began to curse at him, using every four-letter word she could think of. As she called him every name in the book, she said, "I told you to slow down. I told you to stop working all the time. We needed you. I warned you about this. All you did was work. Now you've left me alone with three teen-agers to raise."

Her tears seeped through her anger as she yelled at him and I stood with her in silence. She looked at me and said, "I'm sorry Chaplain, I shouldn't talk like this in front of you."

I replied, "That's alright. Go ahead, tell him." And she did. She returned to cursing him, although with less steam behind her words. Finally her anger quieted and she moved into a volume of tears, em-braced him, and said, "I know you were poor growing up. I know you were afraid we would not have enough. I know that is why you worked so hard." As she worked out her anger and frustration, she moved back and forth between tears, love, anger, appreciation, frustration, and then returned to love again.

Frustration and anger is often expressed or felt toward the one who leaves us. Feeling abandoned, sometimes anger and tears are all we have left to express, at least for a while.

Toward Those Who Do Not Listen

The things that people may say in an attempt to help and encourage us can, in themselves, create frustration and anger. Well-meaning friends may become so busy talking us out of our grief and pain that they do not listen and help us talk out our grief and pain. On some level we know they are doing this because they want to help us feel better, but it frequently causes the grieving person to feel more mis-understood and alone.

Well-meaning friends may become so busy talking us out of our grief and pain that they do not listen and help us talk out our grief and pain.

A widow with young children was experiencing each day as a year and barely managing to get through emotionally. She was trying to be there for her children. She felt frustrated with well-meaning friends because of the way they tried to encourage her. They frequently of-fered comments such as, "You're young. You will find another man to love and love you." Unfortunately the message between the lines was, "Don't hurt. Just feel better." Often the message between the words was, "I cannot handle your pain. I do not know what to say or how to listen, so I want you to act happy" These well-meaning friends were unaware that the best way to help her was to listen, allow her to name the feelings, and help her talk them out, hurt them out, and grieve them out. Perhaps then she could experience some release, understanding, and encouragement and not feel so alone.

After an accident in which Mary's husband died and she lived, friends had various ways of trying to encourage her. Some of the ways friends encouraged created more frustration and more feelings of being misunderstood rather than encouraged. Some tried to convince her that God took her husband because his mission on earth was finished and that her mission on earth was not finished. They said she had more to accomplish. This frustrated her. It was not that she did not believe that there was more to accomplish with her life, but her frustration was felt as she heard them try to explain the mystery of death and suffering. They wanted her to feel better and be encouraged by their explanations. However, this widow only felt more misunderstood, alone, and frustrated. Mary needed someone to listen to her hurting soul.

Another way people try to help is through identification or telling their own stories. George was telling another friend about his abdomen pain, the growth found on the test, and his fear that it was cancer. The well-meaning friend interrupted by telling the story of a friend who had that same problem and it turned out to be nothing. As a result, George stopped talking about his concerns and fears and quickly moved on. He found himself frustrated with this friend for not listening and allowing him to get it off his chest. He needed someone to listen. Perhaps there is no greater love than for a man or woman to close his or her mouth and open his or her ears and eyes, so that another may express himself or herself completely and freely.

Perhaps there is no greater love than for a man or woman to close his or her mouth and open his or her ears and eyes, so that another may express himself or herself completely and freely.

Toward the Ones We Love

We may "take it out" on those we love the most, whether this person is our spouse, child, parent, or friend. Grieving persons may avoid the friends they love because these friends are happy and content with life. After a fetal death or birth of a child with deformity or retardation, the parents may avoid good friends whose babies are normal and healthy. The parents may find themselves feeling angry, sad, or jealous.

Anger can seep out without our being aware, so that closest loved ones are often the objects of its expression. Close relationships often seem more secure. Perhaps the frustration and irritability comes out toward these loved ones because we feel they will not abandon or judge us. Often, we become so caught up in our grief that we do not have the energy to be aware of their needs and feelings.

Perhaps the frustration and irritability comes out toward them because we feel they will not abandon or judge us. Often we become so caught up in our grief that we do not have the energy to be aware of their needs and feelings.

Hurt feelings may lead to thoughts of unfairness, injustice, and jealousy. And these thoughts may vibrate feelings of frustration and anger. Sarcasm may flow or leak. If these feelings leak into the open, we feel guilty. Then we blame ourselves for not being able to cope more constructively. The anger may be spontaneous and reactive. We may have little ability to control it. If a person believes that anger is wrong or a sin, he or she may not express it directly. The person may avoid or withdraw from others instead.

If a person believes that anger is wrong or a sin, he or she may not express it directly. The person may avoid or withdraw from others instead.

This is a difficult time for close loved ones. They may feel helpless in the face of the irritable remarks or passive withdrawal. Feeling helpless and also being human, friends may become defensive or protect themselves from the attacks. Friends or loved ones may begin to avoid the grieving person. This can add to the grief and anger because we feel loved ones have abandoned us.

Feeling helpless and also being human, friends may become defensive or protect themselves from the attacks. Friends or loved ones may begin to avoid the grieving person.

Joe and Suzie had been in the bridge group for years. When Joe died the friends insisted that Suzie still come. She did, but it wasn't easy. She missed Joe more when she was with the group. Suzie began feeling jealous and angry because the others had their spouses. When these well-meaning friends said, "I understand," Suzie wanted to scream back, "You don't understand! You have your husband!" But she did not say it. In fact, she felt guilty for having such thoughts. She was not able to discuss these normal feelings with them. After a few meetings, she never attended the bridge group again. As a result, she felt lonelier and the group began to feel they had done something wrong. Soon the friends felt guilty, then hurt, and then angry with Suzie. They even stopped calling her. This dilemma is sad and so unnecessary. But it happens often because we do not understand grief.

Grief's frustration and anger can affect the whole family. Immediately after their fifteen-year-old son was murdered, the parents worked to give their other thirteen-year-old son, Richard, a lot of support and attention. They wanted to help him through the loss of his brother. Within weeks, however, the parents became overwhelmed with their own grief and began to avoid each other and Richard. They avoided each other because they felt such heavy grief that they could not talk without tears, pain, and frustration seeping through their words. They became impatient and irritable with each other and their son. Richard began to feel he could not make them happy. In fact, in some childlike way, he concluded his parents blamed him for his brother's death.

Obviously, what these people needed most was loving, patient, and secure loved ones who understood grief and could embrace and accept their frustrations without taking it personally. It takes personal security to love someone who is caught in the throws of anger and frustration. It takes family or friends who can give us permission to be angry, release it, and talk about it together.

It takes personal security to love someone who is caught in the throws of anger and frustration. It takes family or friends who can give us permission to be angry, release it, and talk about it together.

Toward the Health Care Team

Facing the mystery of illness and death, we often believe that medical science should heal us from illness and death. When healing does not happen, anger may follow. Feeling angry, family member's may threaten to throw lawsuits at the hospital and its professionals. They may need to express it and get it off their chests. Facing the unknown can often inflame helplessness and frustration. We look to medical science and health care professionals to know all things and heal all things, and we may feel frustrated with them in the absence of healing and cure.

Facing the unknown can often inflame helplessness and frustration. We look to medical science and health care professionals to know all things and heal all things. We may feel frustrated with them in the absence of healing and cure.

The anger and blame may compensate for the helplessness, until we can mobilize out of helplessness. Health care professionals need to understand this so that they do not take this personally and be drawn into defensive behavior. When an angry attack is expressed, it is not helpful for the professional to defend the hospital or the health care team.

I will never forget Mrs. Brown's anger and rage. For a number of weeks the physician was attempting to prepare Mrs. Brown for her husband's death. Together they had had a long journey with cancer. Her husband, Mrs. Brown, and the physician had fought the fight well, reaching remission many times over the years. But this time it seemed he was near the end of his earthly journey. Although no one knew for sure, it appeared that Mr. Brown would die within a week or so. Mrs. Brown would not hear or accept it. In her denial, she became enraged with the physician who had been with them faithfully during this three-year illness.

The physician asked the chaplain to go with him to visit Mr. Brown in the unit and then Mrs. Brown who was in denial and anger. The doctor was anxious about her angry response and hoped I could help her face and accept the reality of her husband's upcoming death. As we sat down in the family conference room the doctor gently explained the situation again.

I could see the anger move across her face as she responded, "No, he is not going to die! You have given up, Doctor! This whole hospital has given up on him! Where is your professional determination, Doctor? Aren't you supposed to keep trying? What new medications are on the market? Have you even tried to find any new treatments? My husband is not going to die! But if he does, you can be sure my attorney will be visiting you, Doctor."

This physician had his "stuff" together. He listened long until it seemed she had released most of the anger. Then he gently reached out and touched her hand that had gathered into a fist and said, "I know you're angry with me. I wish I could do more. It's very hard to accept that he may not make it this time." As I observed this deeply caring and nondefensive physician and hurting enraged wife, I was touched by the doctor's compassion. Mrs. Brown was touched also. Her clenched jaw loosened as tears flowed down her cheeks. For the first time in all these hospitalizations, she wept openly and continued weeping. After the physician said good-bye, I stayed and we talked. We talked about her husband's possible death and their long courageous voyage with cancer.

It is so normal to get frustrated and angry with health care professionals when they seem to fail us at a time we feel so helpless and dependent upon them. I have witnessed occasions when professionals became frustrated with themselves for not being able to heal or control disease. Unfortunately, unlike this doctor, I have on occasions also seen that professionals become defensive, start using medical jargon, and miss the *real* needs of patient or family.

Toward God, the Congregation, and the Clergy

I end this chapter where it began. My lament after Abby's birth was, "Why God? If you are the Creator, Sustainer, and Redeemer of all things, why did you allow my daughter to have retardation?" Often my plea is similar to the psalmist, Job, and Jesus in Gethsemane. "My God, my God, why hast thou forsaken me?"

This anguish prompts a self-inventory in which we examine how we tried to keep the laws of God or be a good person, and now this travesty has fallen upon us. We just cannot add things up so we can feel they are just. We may question, "Is there really a God? If so, how could this have happened?" These thoughts may permeate our minds and soul for awhile.

Persons in pain may "act out" beyond their usual values, boundaries, or personal rules. Angrily we may battle with God. In hurt, we may take inventory of our lives and reflect on how we kept the rules of family, life, or faith. We may question, "What did it get me? My child is dead!" We may go through a period of acting out contrary to our beliefs and values.

Since God is difficult to experience in the flesh, we may transfer our frustration to one who represents God, such as the chaplain, minister, rabbi, priest, other clergy, or even caring friends from the congregation. It is easy for ministers to forget whom they represent and that the anger one has toward God may naturally be expressed toward the minister, who is present in the moment and in the flesh.

Since God is difficult to experience in the flesh, we may transfer our frustration to the ones who represent God, such as the chaplain, minister, rabbi, priest, other clergy, or even caring friends from the congregation.

For awhile, we may withdraw from the congregation because we believe fellow parishioners let us down in some way. They may have come to comfort, but only offered us platitudes. Platitudes and easy answers such as, "Just remember, this is God's will," or "God knows what He is doing," or "Remember, everything works out for good for those who love the Lord, " or "Remember that God never puts more on us than we can handle." As caring people we often try to make people feel better and in doing so we belittle the pain with the quick fix or quick encouragement. A helpful sojourner will be one who allows you to have your pain and to express it to them.

Grieving people need help expressing their anger and frustration to God. Often we feel it's wrong to talk to God with this kind of open and honest anger. We may feel guilty for feeling the way we do and more guilty if we actually express it. These guilty feelings can become the impetus for more isolation and distance from God and His people.

Raise your fist or voice and express your lament to God, if you feel the lament. Express your anger to God, if you feel anger. I believe this is an act of faith and prayer. It is an act of faith in God when we honestly and directly express to God how we feel and where it hurts. In this expression of anger we are mysteriously saying that we believe God "is." We do not express anger toward one we do not believe exists. In expressing the frustration and anger, we are affirming that God is intimately intertwined in our joy and sorrow, yet in such a way that we do not understand where God is. Being a creature can be frustrating in the midst of suffering!

It is an act of faith in God when we honestly and directly express to God how we feel and where it hurts. In this expression of anger we are mysteriously saying that we believe God "is."

If our anger cannot be expressed openly and honestly to God, then we may suppress these feelings until we feel numb and apathetic. The faith statement of anger toward God may say, "You matter to me, but I don't understand you! Where are you?"

Anger is an uncomfortable emotion for most of us. We want so much to let go of the constant sense of frustration and, yet, we cannot. These emotions are important vehicles, which are given to us to help move us through the wilderness of grief. If anger does not find responsible expression and release, it can spoil within and lead to bitterness, isolation, and deeper depression. If we cannot express and talk it through with loved ones and God, then we may become stuck. We may become stuck in bitterness rather than moving toward better.

Chapter 6

Praying for a Miracle

The Spirit is that divine power beyond us that joins a power within us that together can transform and transcend life and death. For me, this is the Spirit of God. Faith in this Spirit can empower us to climb mountains, overcome diseases, and walk the valleys and the shadows of life and death we never thought possible. Faith can miraculously heal and also miraculously help us face death itself.

The Spirit is that divine power beyond us that joins a power within us that together can transform life and death. For me this is the Spirit of God. Faith in this Spirit can empower us to climb mountains, overcome disease, and walk the valleys and shadows of life and death we never thought possible.

When the threat of loss falls upon us, we may naturally pray for a miracle. When cancer is diagnosed, we want a miracle to heal us. When a hurricane gathers and is coming directly toward our city, we pray and hope for a miracle to dissipate the storm. When we have lost a significant love, we pray for God to miraculously take away the pain. There is gift in our reaching and praying for a miracle. It can empower us and lead us to healing.

When the threat of loss falls upon us, we may naturally pray for a miracle.

Numerous research studies demonstrate that faith and prayer can complement medical science and technology to bring about healing, remission of disease and cure. Herbert Benson, Joan Borysenko, Larry Dossey, Harold Koenig, Elisabeth McSherry, and others have pub-

The Unwanted Gift of Grief: A Ministry Approach
© 2006 by The Haworth Press, Inc. All rights reserved.
doi:10.1300/5644_07

lished research demonstrating this powerful faith factor.[1] Faith, prayer, love, attitude, visualization, and meditation can enhance natural healing chemistry in our bodies. Faith in God and God's healing power can bring physical healing and spiritual healing to mind, body and spirit. In the November 10, 2003, issue of *Newsweek,* the cover story was "God & Health: Is Religion Good Medicine? Why Science is Starting to Believe in Faith and Healing" by Claudia Kalb.[2] This article supports what many faith groups have always believed concerning divine intervention for suffering and death.[3] Recent studies demonstrate that the power of prayer and faith positively affects the healing process after injury or surgery and enhances the immune system in fighting disease.

Faith, prayer, love, attitude, visualization, and meditation can enhance natural healing chemistry. Faith in God and God's healing power can bring physical healing and spiritual healing to mind, body, and spirit.

But if the miracle does not come, we may have to rethink our understanding of faith, miracles, cure and healing. This is often the work we do in the wilderness before we enter the transforming journey toward facing death, loss, or fear.

If the miracle does not come we may have to rethink our understanding of faith and miracles. This is often the work we do in the wilderness of grief.

This same faith in miracle can also be used as an attempt to deny death or defend us from the reality of our death and loss. In this defense, we may make promises and contracts with God as a way of obtaining a miracle and avoiding the crosses we must ultimately face.

HOLY AND EARTHLY CONTRACTS: HOPE FOR HEALING AND CURE

During this part of the journey, we often make contracts with God. Contracts are similar to bargains or promises we negotiate with God in order to gain healing or cure in exchange for our best behavior or strong religious practices. Making contracts are a normal part of the grief process and fearing the future. Every pastor who takes the time to deeply listen has heard suffering people wrestle as they make these contracts with God.

Contracts are similar to bargains or promises we negotiate with God in order to gain healing or cure in exchange for our best behavior or strong religious practices. Making contracts are a normal part of the grief process.

Numerous researchers, observers, clergy, nurses, and physicians have witnessed these bargains with God and promises to God. Elisabeth Kübler-Ross, in her research presented in *On Death and Dying,* made us more aware of that which pastors and nurses had witnessed and experienced for centuries.[4] My hope in the paragraphs ahead is to address more specifically the spiritual and religious dimensions of these bargains. I call these "contracts" with God.

Once we become aware of a loss or terminal disease, we may call upon God, the Holy Spirit, the minister, or physician requesting healing, cure, and miracle. We know we have cancer but, on the other hand, we believe that God will cure. Such contracts may be stated as, "I will read scripture, pray, go to worship everyday if you, o God, will heal me." Or it might sound similar to, "God, I know you can perform miracles if my faith is strong enough." Or perhaps it is expressed this way, "Lord, you can make my daughter with mental retardation, normal, if only I have faith and believe more strongly." Human contracts made with the Divine are many and varied.

One can hear in these laments the forming of a negotiation with God, which states that, "If I do this Lord, then, I know, you will do that." The requests may be to "heal this, change this, lift the pain and I will . . ." Deep in the broken heart is a yearning for the miracle we hope God will grant if we knock enough, seek enough, ask enough, or if we are good enough.

Deep in the broken heart is a yearning for the miracle we hope God will grant if we knock enough, seek enough, ask enough, or if we are good enough.

None of us wants to suffer or die. Contracts are a defense against being human. To be human is to know that someday we will die. If I am diagnosed with a terminal illness, I am sure that I, too, will make contracts with God, attempting to plead my case through more devout faithfulness and prayer. This is an authentic part of being human. Yet some day we must face the reality of our death, whether during this particular episode of illness or the next. We will not live forever!

Some day we must face the reality of our death whether during this particular episode of illness or the next. We will not live forever!

MIRACLES AND SAYING "YES" TO DEATH AND SUFFERING

Somehow we must lower our defenses against death and, when our sacred time comes, say "yes" to death and suffering. When our sacred time comes, we must learn to faithfully let go and let be. This does not mean we invite or cause death or suffering. Nor does it mean we should not seek treatment. On the contrary, we must take care of our health and be good stewards of our bodies. We need to pray for healing and search for the best medical care available. Yet someday, we must say "yes" to death.

Reading this, you could prematurely conclude that I do not believe in miracles. You would be wrong to draw that conclusion. Later in this chapter I will write about a time in which daughter, Abby, was miraculously healed by God and God's gift of medicine. I believe that God has the power to do and will do anything God chooses to do. But a miracle is God's doing and is not based on our good behavior or strong faith.

I believe that God has the power to do and will do anything God chooses to do. But a miracle is God's doing and is not based on our good behavior or strong faith.

As a hospital chaplain, I often see the faithful die and the unfaithful live. I witness God-loving people pray for miracles and not receive them. Often, the faithful suffer and the faithless overcome suffering. I continue to observe the biblical truth that it rains on the just and the unjust. As a chaplain and counselor, I walk with the sufferer, pray for the sufferer and try to unbind his or her suffering. Yet, my earnest prayers and his or her earnest prayers may not result in cure.

At times, the faithful suffer and the faithless overcome suffering. I walk with the sufferer and pray for the sufferer. Yet, my earnest prayers and his or her earnest prayers may not result in cure.

Contracts and Feelings of Isolation, Inadequacy, and Guilt

Often I sojourn with people through their dying. Frequently, I have heard them express guilt because they felt their faith and prayers were not strong enough to bring about a miracle from God. When miracles do not happen, they may talk about feeling that God has abandoned them or that their faith was not strong enough. Some may conclude that they have failed in their part of the contract and, therefore, God did not heal or cure them. Incorrectly they may conclude that their faith was not good enough to bargain a miracle. As a result, they may feel isolated, hurt, or angry. They may feel abandoned and alone in the wilderness.

Some sufferers conclude that they failed in their part of the contract and, therefore, God did not heal or cure them. Incorrectly, they conclude that their faith was not good enough or strong enough to bargain a cure.

In more than thirty years as a hospital chaplain, I can count on one hand the times that the patient, family, or doctor announced a miracle cure after the cancer diagnoses had been clearly established. Seldom have I witnessed cure by prayer powers alone. This is after having been with multitudes of faithful people who prayed for a miracle. Many died in spite of their prayers and faithfulness. Guilt, isolation, and loneliness may be the result, if the patient's minister or faith group continues to pray only for physical cure and not be willing to talk about the possibility of death, if the patient needs to do so. Healing is so much more than physical cure.

Guilt, isolation, and loneliness may be the result, if the patient's minister and faith group continues to pray only for physical cure and it does not happen.

Rather than embrace all of Jesus' prayer in the Garden of Gethsemane, the patient, minister, or faith tradition may pray only one side of that prayer. We may pray only the side which pleads that the cup of death be taken away. When the cup does not pass, the dying or suffering person may experience self-depreciation and may conclude that God does not care.

When we were children we naturally had a self-centered or self-focused view of the world. We thought if good things happened, it was because we made them happen by being good. If bad things happened, we concluded we made them happen because we were bad. This self-focused thinking is normal behavior in childhood development. It may reappear in adult trauma, intense fear, or profound pain. In a crisis, adults frequently regress back to childhood feelings and thinking. This is usually caused by fear and anxiety when we pray for the cup to be lifted and it is not, we may too quickly move to childlike explanations. These explanations can conclude that it is because we did not have enough faith. Some may conclude that God does not take the disease or pain away because we were not good enough. Others may conclude that God caused the illness in the first place, because they were not good enough.

Believe in a God of Covenant—Not Contract

The person with a contract view of God tends to perceive The Almighty as one to be negotiated with, rather than perceive The Almighty as a God of covenant. A covenant God is perceived as one who is with us on the mountaintop and also in the valleys of life and death. The person with a contract view of God may make numerous contracts expecting to gain God's love and favorable response on the basis of his or her faithfulness. The person who views God as a covenant God, knows that in the good days and bad, God is with us. We need not negotiate or make deals with this God. We need only to embrace the power of His abiding love for us. This may sometimes cure but will always heal, whether we live or die.

We need not negotiate or make contracts with God. We need only to embrace the power of His abiding love for us. God's love can sometimes cure but will always heal, whether we live or die.

I met Patricia in the hospital three years after she was diagnosed with cancer. Her church placed considerable emphasis on praying for a miracle. This belief was held strongly by Patricia and her congregation. Everyone told her that if she just kept the faith a miracle would cure the cancer. In the past three years, she had surgery, radiation, and chemotherapy and now was back in the hospital with more complications. In this hospitalization, her physician did not hold out hope for remission. In her forties, Patricia had much to live for and prayed diligently and fervently that God would grant her a miracle.

Patricia's pastor told her that if she put away all doubt, God would heal. He told her not to give opportunity for the devil to interrupt God's healing promises. The entire church prayed for a curing miracle.

Patricia shared with me that in the early months of her illness, she prayed faithfully and read the Bible repeatedly. She had held on with all her might to the pastor's promise and God's promise of a miracle. She believed it would happen, if she did not doubt God's power. I listened carefully as Patricia told me the story of her illness, faith, and the congregation's prayers. Not once did she share openly with me her anxiety or doubt about not receiving a miracle. Yet her doubt seemed to leak out between her words. As the weeks progressed, her body did not heal. In fact, she got worse. She grew weaker and the cancer grew stronger.

Patricia was faithful to the teachings of her church and I did not challenge her beliefs. Her beliefs were important to her at the time. These beliefs helped push away the reality of her illness and possible death. They gave her hope for cure.

As our relationship developed, she began to trust me more. Patricia began to share her doubt more openly. She doubted out loud if God would heal her this time. She began to believe that death might be ahead. Patricia confessed that she felt guilty because in saying this to me, she thought that this meant she was not a faithful person. She felt she was not only letting God down by not keeping faith in a miracle, but felt she was letting down her family, pastor, and congregation. Patricia wept as she shared this with me.

Continuing to weep, Patricia confessed that her faith was not strong enough. She felt abandoned because God did not love her enough to grant her a miracle. "Maybe my faith is just not good enough or maybe I am not good enough," she said as I listened. Patricia went on, "My friends and pastor keep telling me to believe and I don't believe anymore. I believe that I am going to die. Does this mean I have failed God—because I don't believe anymore that God will cure me?"

I responded, "No, Patricia, you are a deeply faithful person. You remind me of Jesus in Gethsemane."

Patricia looked puzzled as I sat in silence after my comment. Finally she asked, "What do you mean?"

I went on, "You remind me of Jesus in Gethsemane when he prayed all night for a miracle and did not receive it. He prayed for the Father to take the cup of suffering and death from him and His father did not. Patricia, whether you live or die, God is with you. Your cure does not depend on how much faith you have or don't have. You are carved in the palm of God's hand."

Patricia wept tears of relief. Now her tears were not of guilt, inadequacy, or because God had abandoned her, Patricia wept because she realized she could die knowing that God was for her not against her. She felt God's grace rather than judgment, God's presence not distance. In her dying days ahead, she began to feel God's presence and believed that God would walk with her through the cross of cancer and death.

This story is not meant to be critical of faith communities that profoundly believe in miracles. God can heal and cure. However, God's healing power does not depend on how faithful or good we are. If that were so, we all would be a day late and a prayer short. God's covenant with us is that whether we live, die, or grieve, God is with us. God is closer than our own breath.

God can heal and cure. But God's healing power does not depend on how faithful or good we are. If that were so, we all would be a day late and a prayer short. God's covenant is that God is closer than our own breath.

Some of Patricia's family and congregation members started witnessing a different kind of miracle. They witnessed her experiencing the miracle of faith that said "yes" to death. She courageously said good-bye to family and loved ones and navigated the transforming journey through dying into death. She faithfully went through the painful labor and contractions of dying as she reentered the eternal womb of God. What a faith! What a miracle! I often wonder if I will have this abiding faith when my day comes to say "yes" to death and meet my maker.

This state of faith is not easy to hold on to. In fact, it is a constant wrestle in the wilderness. Remember, that this faith is filled with labor, contractions, fears, and anxieties, but it is also filled with courage, hope, and peace. Slowly we embrace that God is with us whether we live or die. This God of covenant cries and laughs with us.

Slowly we embrace that God is with us whether we live or die. This God of covenant cries and laughs with us.

You wonder if I believe in miracles? Yes, I believe in miracles! I have walked with these people who have a covenant faith. I have witnessed their suffering and deaths. It is a miracle to me that they are able to courageously face their dying and take the sting out of death through faith. They participate in one of God's miracles. Yet, not a miracle in the way we often think of a miracle. We usually think of a miracle as complete physical cure, and certainly that is miraculous. Healing that comes through the joining of medicine and faith is miraculous. But I must tell you, that a greater miracle that I have witnessed has been the faith and courage that these treasured patients embodied as they carried their diseases and faced their deaths. It is a miracle to me that one can faithfully say "yes" to death when that sacred time come and make the journey to God's eternal breast and rest.

I must tell you, that a greater miracle that I have witnessed has been the faith and courage that these treasured patients embodied as they carried their diseases or faced their deaths.

Faith in miracles is not just expressing half of the Gethsemane prayer, "Abba, take this cup from me!" and the cup be miraculously taken away. Miracle and faith are expressing and living out the second half of the prayer as well. That is, "not my will but Thy will be done." Yet even then, just like Jesus, we may experience the same sense of isolation and abandonment and cry out, "Why hast thou forsaken me?" (Matthew 26, 27:46, RSV).

Miracle and faith is expressing and living out the second half of the Gethsemane prayer as well. That is, "not my will, but Thy will be done." Yet even then, just like Jesus, we may experience the same sense of isolation and abandonment and cry out, "Why hast thou forsaken me?" (Matthew 26, 27:46 RSV)

November 14, 1973, was the darkest day of my young life. My daughter, Abby, was born with Down syndrome. My faith was shaken by the chaos caused by the splitting of her twenty-first chromosome. Abby would forever be mentally handicapped.

The next day in the midst of shock, anguish, and disbelief, a friend said something that startled me. But, my response startled me more. He said to me, "Tim, I believe in miracles. I am going to pray that God heal Abby and make her normal."

I pondered his comment for long, searching moments. I yearned that it could be true. I yearned that Abby could miraculously be made "normal." Then my shaken spirit steadied and I responded, "I just can't pray for that kind of miracle. I pray for a miracle that God will give me the faith and courage to accept Abby for who she is. I pray that God will help me love her right where she is, so I can help her grow and develop to her fullest potential."

I have reflected many times on that bold statement of long ago. I have anguished many days with the question, "Why can't she be normal, autonomous, and an independent person like her younger siblings?" If God had miraculously healed Abby, life would have been so much easier. Yet, the greater miracle may be that we as a family loved and accepted Abby and have walked with her faithfully on the journey of life. Still a greater miracle has been that we have each learned from Abby how to unconditionally love.

The Hope for Healing and Cure

There is a great paradox here. Where negotiations and contracts with God can cause us to miss the truth that God is with us in good days and bad, at the same time, these interactions can lead us to important healing pathways. Our defense against death and the wish to live, can in themselves guide us to sources of healing through science, medicine, faith, spirituality, and God.

Our defense against death and the wish to live, can in themselves guide us to sources of healing through science, medicine, faith, spirituality, and God.

Yet, the danger is that this faith may cause us to approach medicine or God in such a way that it interrupts our facing the wilderness of grief or death. As a result we may not face grief and death openly with loved ones. Instead, we may avoid loved ones and avoid finishing life's business together. We may not name our love and good-byes for one another. Because of our inability to say "yes" to death, we may misuse or overuse medical technology and resources in an attempt to extend our life beyond our sacred moment for death. In some patient situations today, medical technology is being used irresponsibly to prolong death rather than prolong life.

Many suffering people join their faith in God with medicine and find longer life and remission or cure of disease. But when a miracle fails to happen, we often fail to believe that God is with us. Rather than place the options for God's realness on the bargaining table of our physical healing, we need a faith in a covenant God who can physically and spiritually cure, as well as, walk with us in suffering and death when physical cure does not happen. This is the great difference in healing and curing. Healing can restore and give us courage to face death, carry our loss, or disease. Curing, on the other hand, removes the illness.

Rather than place the options for God's realness on the bargaining table of our physical healing, we need a faith in a covenant God who can physically and spiritually cure, as well as walk with us in suffering and death when physical cure does not happen.

Whether physically cured or spiritually healed, we need to reach for a covenant faith, which holds the truth that we are carved in the palm of God's hand whether we live or die. Whether we go to the mountaintop or the valley, God is with us. This truth will set us free.

We need to hold to a belief that each of us is carved in the palm of God's hand whether we live or die. This truth will set us free.

MOM'S GOOD DEATH

Mom and Dad went camping with other snowbirds from all over the country. Mom had a stroke and was rushed to the hospital. By the time I arrived, the doctors had been quite frank that this was a very serious mid-stem brain hemorrhage and that they were amazed she was still alive. Both her hands were twisted and partially paralyzed. To all our amazement, she was mentally alert and competent. She was able to talk with a slight slur and was surprisingly articulate in each conversation in the ICU. The greatest concern she expressed was her worry that Dad was not eating right and taking care of himself.

Dad and I talked with the doctors and nurses about DNR (do not resuscitate) and allowing natural death (AND). My mother did not want to be on a life-sustaining machine and my father was in full agreement not to give her any resuscitation if, indeed, she arrested and her heart stopped. As I remember this, I realize that these were not difficult decisions. As a pastor, Dad had seen many situations and crises such as this. He had witnessed many people die. But also as a pastor, he had witnessed many of his people be connected to machines for weeks and even months before death. My parents were quite clear on this issue. They wanted to do all that could me done medically without CPR or other dramatic means of continuing life or postponing death.

After a week or so in the ICU, Mom got stronger but her paralysis was still quite severe. The medical goal after a stroke is to have the patient start rehabilitation as soon as possible. This creates the best chances for the return of body functions. So when she was stable, we transported her by ambulance to a hospital closer to home. There, she began physical rehabilitation in the hospital where I served.

Mom started that rehab program with determination. She asked Dad to buy her some new tennis shoes to work out in. She told me she was going to overcome this stroke. The therapists began teaching her how to swallow, walk, and use her hands again.

A few days after she arrived, I went by again to visit her. Actually I had been in the hospital early that morning to teach a seminar on death, dying, and grief. (Wow, life is a mystery.) Having finished my seminar, I thought I would run up to the floor and see Mom before going to my son's basketball game. I never made it to the game.

Mom spotted me down the hall about the same time I spotted her. She was in her wheelchair with Dad pushing her around the hallway. When she saw me, she raised both twisted hands in the air to say hello. We greeted. Mom told me about rehab and her hard work. I noticed her paralyzed foot kept falling out of the wheelchair stirrup. Dad and I kept putting her foot back in the stirrup.

Mom was tired and she told me so. "I feel so tired. They are working me hard," she said with exhaustion. Two or three minutes later she told me again she was tired. Mom then leaned back in her chair, closed her eyes, and took her last peaceful breath on earth. Before my eyes, Mom died as we were talking. It all happened in less than a minute.

I got the nurse and she moved Mom back to the room, and lifted her limp body back on to the bed. With Dad on one side of the bed and me on the other, we stood in silent shock for a moment. The nurse said, "I think you know what is happening. I know that you did not want anything done if this happened. Is that still what you want?" With a glance at Dad and a nod between us, we communicated to the nurse that we did not want anything else done. We wanted to let go and let God.

As Dad held his sweetheart of forty-three years and cried, I talked and walked with Mom into death. I said to her, "It's okay Mom, go ahead and die. Go ahead and be with God." I was choking in my tears. There was a long pause as Dad talked and cried.

I continued, "You have loved us and it's okay for you to go to be with God. Dad is right here and he loves you. I am here and I love you. Phil [my oldest brother] loves you. David [my middle brother] loves you. All the grandkids love you. You have loved us. It's okay to go be with God."

I will never forget that intimate time of dying and death with my mother. Dad and I faithfully walked with her into death. Like midwive's, we were there to encourage and coach her last labor on earth. We watched, encouraged, and supported her, as she went through her last labor and contractions into new life and eternal life with her Maker.

I am so grateful to Mom for dying when Dad and I were present. She gave us a painful and powerful gift. I will cherish those moments and memories all the days of my life. She died a good death.

ADVANCE DIRECTIVES AND DNR ORDERS

We need to do all we can to live. But when the sacred time comes, we need to say "yes" to death. With faith, we need to let go and let be—let go and let God. We need to take the sting out of our perceptions of death and faithfully let death become a part of life. We need to develop and sign our advance directives, now. We need to make decisions now about medical technology, DNR, CPR, and allowing natural death. If you do not know about these procedures and forms that require your signature, talk to your doctor, minister, a hospital chaplain, nurse, or lawyer. Then put them in your medical record and glove compartment of your car. Give them to all your children. This will help them make decisions that follow your wishes.

ABBY'S GOOD MIRACLE

When we bring our best faith and the best of medicine together, miracles can happen. Abby continues to be my teacher. I must say though, I hope that she will not continue to teach me in the following frightening way.

Abby is in her early thirties. She is short, muscular, and has long blonde hair. Abby works out every week with her own personal trainer. She works in the hospital wellness center and loves her work. I think she knows everyone in the hospital by name.

Over the years she has participated in every Special Olympics event and presently finds bowling her favorite. For relaxation, she volunteers at the hospital, listens to music, dances, sings with her karaoke machine, types on her computer, talks endlessly on the phone, and keeps up with her siblings. Abby is tough as nails because she had to survive life with her brothers and sisters who love her and protect her and, at the same time, expect a lot from her.

When Abby was twenty-six, we took her to the emergency room with what we thought was a severe cold and at most simple pneumonia. She was admitted to the hospital overnight for antibiotic treatments and observation. Frequently she had a panic on her face because she could not get her breath.

On the second day, Abby was admitted to the ICU. I thought this was just for closer monitoring but the medical staff seemed suddenly in a hurry. In ICU we met with a pulmonary specialist. The team of nurses, physicians, laboratory technicians, and respiratory therapists were all running in every direction bringing breathing machines, monitors, and other technologies into Abby's room. Even I, a hospital chaplain, could not understand what was happening except that it was happening fast.

After attaching the oxygen monitor to Abby, the doctor watched the monitor and within minutes, asked us to step outside the ICU room and said, "Abby is not going to give us much more time." Her lungs were filling with fluid rapidly. He requested our permission to put her on a breathing machine.

As the breathing machine was coming toward her, her mother was holding Abby's hand at the bedside. Abby's face had fear written all over it. Her mother needed to step back to allow more room for the monitors and technology. Abby said to her, "Mommy, I am scared. I am scared I am going to die."

Recognizing Abby's fear and yet knowing the staff need to move technology next to her bed, the doctor asked, "Abby, can I hold your hand?" Slowly Abby let go of her mother's hand and held on to the doctor's as we watched from a distance.

With medications, they induced her into a sleep state so that she would not panic or fight the breathing machine. For the first time in almost twenty-four hours, she let go and was in a relaxed state of chemically created sleep. When this was accomplished, the doctor asked us to step outside again for a family conference. Obviously, we had by now realized that something very, very serious was happening in Abby's body.

We learned that the pneumonia was progressive and severe. Her lungs were filling up quickly. With compassion, yet clarity, the doctor told us that Abby was probably going to die that same day. Unbelievable! We had no idea we were staring at death. We could not believe what we were hearing.

The doctor went on to tell us that he could only suggest one possibility and that possibility would only give Abby a 1 percent chance to live. He suggested that we connect Abby to an ECMO (extracorporeal membrane oxygenation) heart-lung transfusion machine. The ECMO was a huge *Star Wars*–looking piece of technology. Its task was to take Abby's blood out of her body and bypass the lungs, which now were barely functioning. The ECMO would then oxygenate the blood as the lungs would have done and put the oxygenated blood back into her body.

It was also the doctor's responsibility to inform us of the risk, side effects, or negative outcomes. They were severe and scary. He explained that this was a relatively unknown treatment process under these particular circumstances and especially with Abby's age and size. He told us that usually this method only works for four or five days before other organs begin to break down. He hoped in five days the lungs would clear, but also the risk of the treatment was very clear.

The doctor ended by saying, "Please understand, this is your choice and even if we try it, Abby will probably die anyway. We only have a one percent chance! Do you understand what I am saying?"

I must confess I had been around medical technology too long. I silently had severe doubts and questions in my mind. Over the years, I had witnessed amazing positive results and I had witnessed amazing negative results from the use of life-sustaining technology. As my mind raced, I could not get clear for myself which path to take. We had to decide quickly in order to get the technology, technologists, and surgeons available to attach the ECMO to Abby's little body. Fortunately, Abby's mother quickly concluded we would take the ECMO and the 1 percent chance. This R2D2 (as I named it) of the medical technoworld was brought in within hours and the journey of waiting began. This R2D2 was like an angel that brought us more time for healing.

While Abby lay in her chemical sleep, we experienced thoughts and emotions of fear, confusion, helplessness, faithlessness, desperation, and also we felt determined, hopeful, faithful, courage, and always profound love for Abby. We moved back and forth between the family waiting room and her bedside, talking to her, reassuring her, and touching her, while not knowing if she really heard a word we said. The tears were many and we vacillated between hope and despair, courage and fear, and faith and faithlessness. At times, I felt like a two- or three-year-old child trying to grasp the unbelievable happening around me. Prayers did not seem to go beyond the ceiling. I could only think, "Why God? Why have you forsaken Abby?"

Adult siblings and family arrived. Each carried their sorrow and hope. Each had their own way of grieving and for sure each had many questions. We walked the halls. We sat. We went in the ICU to talk to Abby. We walked the halls. We sat. We went in to talk to Abby. Over the next four days we took turns with the vigil, received support from friends and colleagues, heard funny stories about Abby that we had never heard before, and then laughed again and cried again. The prayers from others saturated our awareness.

On the second day we brought her Walkman and put the headset on with her favorite music. We brought in one of her Special Olympics gold medals and hung it on the wall. We continued to talk to her and encourage her.

Before a Special Olympics game the athletes are asked to recite a pledge. The pledge ends with the athletes saying together, "and if I cannot win, let me be brave in the attempt." We wanted Abby to show us a sign that she was winning this fight to live, but we knew that she was being brave in the attempt. The question was not her bravery, but our bravery. Could we be brave in the attempt if Abby would not win in this race for her life?

Every morning we not only waited for the physicians to make rounds, but we waited for the X-rays. It became our daily ritual of measuring if there was any hope. For three mornings the X-rays showed that the fluid in the lungs continued to fill. Abby was getting dramatically worse and so were our spirits.

Soon the predicted negative side effects began showing up. On the second day, she began to hemorrhage. By the third day, her kidneys were losing function. All of this happened in spite of R2D2's help. Her blood pressure danced dangerously up and down. All the family, staff, and friends waited in prayerful yearning. We all wanted a positive sign from Abby's body and from her determined spirit. But the positive signs did not come.

The third morning the chest X-rays showed that her lungs were almost totally filled with pneumonia. On that same evening we were approached by a nurse and close personal friend. She asked us to consider a DNR order. This was hard to hear and even more difficult to consider. We knew it was a message from the staff that said Abby was profoundly losing ground. We finally signed the document with clear instructions to do everything to help her, except to not give Abby electrical CPR. We did not want her little body to suffer any more.

On that same evening we talked about memorial services for Abby. We knew that some family had to return home, but also we wanted to prepare the brothers and sisters for what we thought was ahead. We wanted them to be a part of planning the services. In tears and laughter the family talked and planned. It was clear that this service was going to be a real celebration of Abby's life and our love for her.

After this difficult decision, the family gathered in the hospital chapel and prayed together. We prayed words of gratitude for Abby and her life with us. We prayed that she be healed. We prayed for a miracle. We prayed that she not have to suffer. We prayed, that if she could not be healed, that we find the courage to face her death. Slowly in solitude and with hugs, we left the chapel to get some much-needed rest, so we could wait again the next day.

Around 4:30 a.m. Abby's nurse called the house. She said we should come quickly because Abby's blood pressure was dropping dramatically. I drove on to the hospital ahead of the rest of the family. As I backed out of the driveway, I shouted at God. "God, don't let her suffer. Either let her die or heal her, but don't let her suffer!" If anybody had been in the car with me, I am sure they would have been embarrassed, shocked, or waiting for lightning to strike. My shouting prayer was from the gut and not flowered with reverence. I was angry, demanding, and pleading, all in the same shout.

When we arrived at the hospital, Abby's blood pressure had bounced back. We were relieved and confused. I think in this early morning event, I came to the full realization that Abby was not going to make it. Rather than go home and get a shower, we decided to wait for the chest X-rays to come in.

When the doctor arrived, we all gathered by the X-ray screen as we had every morning. We could not believe it! Abby's lungs were clear! Not partially clear, but totally clear. At first we thought they had the wrong X-rays, but these were Abby's lungs. They were clear! They were clear! Thank God, they were clear! Wow! I could not believe it! What joy!

Suddenly, I felt more anxious and worried than I had since the first day of putting her on the ECMO machine. All along, one of my biggest fears was that Abby would be brain damaged or remain in a coma. Could she make it off the machine on her own?

The doctor called us in to Abby's bedside and slowly eased her out of the paralysis with medications. The most important sign we waited and watched for was Abby's ability to trigger the machine with her own lungs. Nothing happened. Abby stared off in a daze and was not able to trigger the machine nor recognize us. My heart sank! The doctor induced the paralysis again and she went back under and closed her eyes. Downhearted and fearful, we went to the waiting room to continue our mysterious vigil.

Within an hour, the doctor had tried again to raise her up again and see if she could trigger the breathing machine on her own will. He announced with a big smile that "Abby did it!" We rushed to the ICU room. Abby's eyes were open and seemed dazed, but she was triggering the machine on her own. I moved into her vision and suddenly her pupils moved to follow me. She was responding to our presence and after a while she was responding to our voices and commands. Abby was Abby again. This was a miracle!

After many days in the hospital and a month or so of rehabilitating her weak muscles, Abby was on the way again. Soon, she went back to work at the hospital, started working out with her personal trainer at the Wellness Center, and resumed Special Olympics bowling.

I am grateful for so much! Grateful for our physicians, the hospital staff, for medical science, for a risk taken, for multitudes of friend's prayers, for Abby's determined spirit and body, and for our Heavenly Great Physician. I had come to the point of saying "yes" to death— letting go and letting be—only to discover that in letting go, a miracle was given and Abby was given back to us.

I need to tell you that I have not shouted down the halls or stood on the rooftops to shout out that God gave us a miracle. I have tried to reflect on why. I am intensely grateful to God for the miracle of His healing spirit and medical science. I am grateful, yet I have known good and faithful people who prayed for a miracle and did not receive one. They lost their loved ones in spite of their prayers and hope for a miracle. I was humbled and I could not wave a God-given gold medal miracle in the face of others. I had prayed with many of them and they did not receive a miracle or cure.

Even though I still do not understand, I am grateful. Indeed, miracles are God's doing and are not based on our perfect faith or perfect prayers. Miracles are mysteriously given.

Chapter 7

Wrestling with Sadness and Depression

In the wilderness there are bouts with sadness and, at times, bouts with the full force of depression. This can be experienced in many ways. It can range from the blahs, blues, inability to concentrate, weeping, lack of motivation or interest, and the profound inability to eat, sleep, or function. From time to time all of these may be a part of the grieving process. But we need to take extra care if we, or someone we love, is moving toward deep depression.

In the wilderness there are bouts with sadness and, at times, bouts with the full force of depression. This can be experienced in many ways.

SADNESS AND DEPRESSION: NORMAL PARTS OF HEALING

We invited good friends Aaron and Sarah over for dinner. They had not felt like getting out lately. I felt good about the fact they finally said yes to our invitations. Two months before, they had given birth to a beautiful baby boy born with the cord wrapped around his neck. The physician could not hear the heartbeat. So Sarah went through a lengthy induced labor knowing that the infant in her womb was already dead. Aaron had stayed faithfully with her in labor and delivery.

We were pleased that they accepted the invitation but knew they were grieving. Sarah's previously pregnant body was contracting back into shape. As we visited over appetizers, Sarah was not herself. Her face never changed from a disinterested expression throughout the evening. There was an emotional flatness in her face and voice.

The Unwanted Gift of Grief: A Ministry Approach
© 2006 by The Haworth Press, Inc. All rights reserved.
doi:10.1300/5644_08

She seemed to gaze past us rather than to focus on the one speaking. Dark shadows peaked from under her makeup. Aaron tried to be helpful and carry the load of socialization, but his was a half-hearted effort.

The one who does not understand grief might have concluded that this couple did not want to be there. One may have concluded that it was time for this couple to move on and "enjoy life, try again, or look to the future." The truth is Sarah and Aaron did not want to be there. For that matter, they did not want to be anywhere except with their baby boy. For the time being, Sarah and Aaron's sad and depressed state was the only way they could feel close to their baby.

I asked Sarah how she was making it through. As I expected, her first response was a vague "Okay." As I persisted, she recognized that I really wanted to know. Finally she put into tears and words the pain she tried to protect us from. She said that since little Jeremy died, he was all she could think about. She reported that she wasn't able to sleep much and had little appetite. She had lost weight quickly after giving birth but some of that was related to her lack of interest in food. Although she needed to get things done at home, she often sat and stared with little motivation to do anything or to even talk with friends. On occasion, she woke up in the middle of the night hearing her baby cry and then realized he was not there. As she put into words her profound grief, tears continued to fall. Frequently, she apologized for not being much fun and ruining the party.

Sarah was experiencing significant sadness and depression, which is normal after a significant loss. For nine months she had bonded and nurtured Jeremy through her body. It made sense that her depression was experienced differently and perhaps more profoundly than that of her husband, Aaron.

After a loss, the intensity of sadness and depression is often in relationship to the intensity, significance, and involvement with the person we lose. It made sense that Sarah's bond with her baby was different from the bond felt by her husband, who waited for gestation and delivery. Not only did Sarah not want to go through the labor and contractions to deliver their dead baby, she did not want to go through the labor and contractions of sadness and depression either.

The intensity of sadness and depression is often in relationship to the intensity, significance, and involvement with the person we lose.

This was true in spite of the fact that these labor and contractions would lead to healing. Aaron and Sarah's grief was unwanted and did not feel like a gift at all. They could not in any way understand that the pathway of their sadness and depression would lead to healing and transformation.

Sadness and depression is the body's autonomic nervous system expressing gratitude for the relationship and bond one experienced with another. The word autonomic means it is involuntary. Sadness and depression may include emotional, cognitive, behavioral, and spiritual experiences of dejection and sorrow ranging from mild discouragement and downheartedness to feelings of utter hopelessness and despair.

Sadness and depression may include emotional, cognitive, behavioral, and spiritual experiences of dejection and sorrow ranging from mild discouragement and downheartedness to feelings of utter hopelessness and despair.

Adjustment after a loss may include sadness, dejection, anxiety, guilt, abandonment, anger, loneliness, pessimism, or worry. Rejection may be experienced especially in divorce, suicide, and job loss. One may experience behavioral changes such as: loss of appetite, loss of energy, crying, withdrawal, hyperactivity, or agitation/impatience. Or one might experience gloom, mourning, or sudden tears and emotion when least expected.

Depression is the darkness before the dawn. The darkness may take more than a few months or even years. When one moves into depression, it often means that he or she is moving to accept the fact that what has happened will not change or go away.

Depression is the darkness before the dawn.

Lack of Understanding by Others

Our culture puts dramatic emphasis on being energetic, successful, youthful, happy, positive, and witty. We permit the sufferer to be sad at the funeral, but in a few weeks, or at most a few months, unfortunately we expect the person to be getting on with life and setting new goals.

The work of depression and sadness is similar to the churning of the cream before it can curd and transform into butter. Depression needs to be churned, felt, talked out, and worked out until it transforms into new life. But frequently the people around the depressed person want to rush the spirit and the soul's work and get on to the finished product of happiness.

The work of depression and sadness is similar to the churning of cream before it can curd and transform into butter. Depression needs to be churned, experienced, talked out, and worked out until it transforms us into new life.

Traveling through death and resurrection takes time, but unfortunately we often don't seem to understand the time and work involved. Our best friends may try to cheer us up and make us feel better. Soon, they may stop visiting or calling because they feel uncomfortable with our sad mood and broken spirit. They may feel helpless in knowing what to say.

Our best friends may try to cheer us up and make us feel better. Often this is not helpful.

Identifying the Characteristics of Depression

In sadness and depression there is a deep sense of gloom. These are the dark nights of the soul. We may wrestle with these nights of the soul many times before dawn comes. Consumed with the thoughts of our lost love, every activity may remind us of him or her. An inability to concentrate permeates most events and may interrupt our ability to focus or work. We may become preoccupied with "things" or "memories" of the lost one, go to the cemetery regularly, or play favorite music that reminds us of him or her. Going through belongings, we may reflect and cry over the memories engendered by each treasured piece of jewelry, clothing, or other memento.

In the beginning, we are often consumed with thoughts of our lost love. Every activity may remind us of him or her. An inability to concentrate permeates most events and may interrupt our ability to focus or work.

Often depressed persons drop out of life because it is too painful to socialize. We try to act like we are having a good time, but it can be exhausting trying to keep up the facade. We may avoid social engagements because in the past we shared them with our deceased spouse. Often we can't bear to go to church, parties, or other events because they remind us of the loss we do not want to face. We wonder if we will ever stop crying in the middle of the night or if we will ever laugh again and mean it. We ask, "Will I ever feel like me again? Will the darkness ever lift?"

Everyone experiences sadness and depression differently and responds to it differently. It's not uncommon for some grieving persons to get busy and overwork. They may try to avoid the sadness and depression by overcommitting and filling up all the dark nights of the soul with work and activities.

Some grieving persons may try to avoid the sadness and depression by overcommitting themselves and filling up all the dark nights of the soul with work and activities.

Rushing Through or Avoiding the Desert of Depression

Many may try to rush through or avoid the desert of depression. Usually the fastest and most effective way out of depression and sadness is *through* it. Not around the desert, not over the desert, not under the desert; but *through* the desert of depression.

Usually the fastest and most effective way out of sadness and depression is through *it, not around the desert, not over the desert, not under the desert; but* through *the desert of depression.*

In the desert, we will find growth and renewal. In the desert, we will hear the still small voice of God or the nudge of the Holy Spirit, which will guide us to strength, wisdom, hope, future, and healing. By going into the desert, I do not mean that we isolate ourselves or withdraw from the world. I mean that we allow the pain to be experienced, as it needs to be experienced. We allow our tears expression. Our tears need release and will speak to us in the midst of the release. Our sadness wants expression and this same sadness wants to comfort us. The more we avoid and run from depression the tighter and longer its grip. We need to let the desert and the wilderness transform us.

In the desert we will find growth and renewal. In the desert we will hear the still small voice of God or the nudge of the Holy Spirit, which will guide us to strength, wisdom, hope, future, and healing.

The unwanted gift of sadness and depression often never gets utilized. God and the Spirit wish to embrace us in the pain. However, when our pain and tears surface, we often run away into busyness. Rather than stay too busy, we need to schedule time each day to go to the desert, feel the feelings, and reflect on our loss.

Sadness and Depression Are Similar to . . .

The wrestle with depression is difficult to describe, but let me try. Remember that each person describes this experience differently. I will use the image of being in a cave or dark tunnel. Depression, after a profound loss, is similar to entering a dark tunnel or cave. It is so dark we may not see our hands or feet in the darkness, nor do we know where to place them in order to keep moving through the darkness. We notice that stopping along the way, does give us a bit of rest and a time to cry, but we keep on searching for light. As if using braille with hands and feet, we feel along the walls of the cave and the walls of our soul in order to decide what direction to take.

After many nights, days, and sometimes weeks and months in the darkness, we take a turn and suddenly see off in the distance a brief light. Our step and hope quicken. We breathe faster in hopeful anticipation. We have been in the dark night of the soul so long we had forgotten what hope felt like. At times, we do not realize that we feel a little better until later or the next day. It is similar to realizing, "For a few minutes, I felt good yesterday."

We realize that we had been in the dark night of the soul so long, we had forgotten what hope felt like. At times we do not realize that we feel a little better until later or the next day. It is similar to realizing, "For a few minutes, I felt good yesterday."

In the Desert, God May Seem Far Away

In this state, it is often difficult to experience God's presence. God is often felt as distant or absent. The Holy One may seem transcendent, beyond, far away, or voiceless. Not being able to experience God out there beyond us, we often withdraw into our soul's inner sanctuary. We go deep into this inner sanctuary and, at some point, we may intuit, sense, feel, or perhaps hear the still small voice of God or the slight nudge of the Spirit. Our hope and healing quicken.

In depression, we go deep into the inner sanctuary of our soul and, at some point, we may intuit, sense, feel, or perhaps hear the still small voice of God or the slight nudge of the Spirit. Our hope and healing quicken.

Before, we did not believe that God was with us. But now, in the soul's inner sanctuary, we discover that the Spirit of God is immanently and intimately with us, even closer than our own breath.

When we begin to heal, we often don't realize the healing movements. We may come to the subtle awareness that "This morning I woke up without tears" "Yesterday I wanted to cook again," or "For just a moment yesterday, I felt a sense of peace come over me for no particular reason." These are statements expressed or felt by one who is moving through the desert of darkness, sadness and depression toward light.

The Mysterious Gift of Sadness and Depression

So what is the gift of sadness and depression? We know for sure that we don't want the sadness and depression. But let me try to describe the gift. Mystery is always difficult to explain or put into words.

By going into the desert, we often leave the rational and enter spirit and mystery. Mystery does not make rational sense. In the desert we "let go" of what we hold on to so tightly in our lives. We let go of the one we lost. We let go of the way life was. We let go of yesterday.

By letting go, we enter mystery. Our thinking gives up to emotions and feelings. Our tears may release and flow. Our masks and facades give up to transparency. Our adult logic gives up to regressing into feelings of a child state again. The rational self gives up to wonder. Our need to control gives up to letting go and letting be. Our awareness of temporal time gives up to eternal awareness. We let go of the way life has been and, as a result, our life is transformed toward depth, height, breadth, and newness.

Our spirit is transformed toward healing and wholeness. All things become "new," yet, we still know the old. We are grasped by the Spirit and participate in a faith, which sees through things, people, sadness, despair, and depression with new eyes.

Our spirit is transformed toward healing and wholeness. All things become "new," yet, we still know the old. We are grasped by the Spirit and participate in a faith, which sees through things, people, sadness, and depression with new eyes.

MOVEMENT INTO LIGHT AND HEALING

In this movement toward light, we know on an unexplainable spiritual level that the one we lost in death was a temporal and temporary gift. Yet, we know that his or her role and spirit in the drama of our lives enfleshed a love and presence that was a gift from God—the eternal love and spirit. In the desert of depression and sadness all things are being made ultimately new, ultimately healed, ultimately whole and holy. Through this painful wrestling, we began to differentiate and individuate toward new being. We let go and transform. We internalize the truth. This was a truth we knew all along but could not fully grasp. This truth is that all things are gift but are also temporary. We are invited to die to the old in order to rise up to new life. This process is painful, yet leads to transformation.

In this wrestle, we enter the experience of the Garden of Gethsemane. We embrace the cross and move toward resurrection. Our anxieties embrace peace. Our fears embrace courage, our doubts embrace faith, our despair embraces hope, our broken life begins to heal, and our grief is finding direction. We are being made new. We are living toward resurrection.

In this wrestle our anxieties embrace peace, our fears embrace courage, our doubts embrace faith, our despair embraces hope, and our broken life begins to heal. Our grief is finding direction. We are being made new. We are living toward resurrection.

If we allow ourselves to enter the unwanted gift of sadness and depression, we will cross the desert. The spiritual muscle of character, endurance, courage, and hope, which we develop in this wilderness, will carry us through. It will carry us through when life's deserts come again. It will carry us through to new joys.

I realize that what I have written here is heavy stuff. Please do not be concerned if this has not been your experience or if you don't understand what I am trying to say. We all experience grief differently. You have your own metaphors, symbols, feelings, and words for describing your wilderness and your healing process. Spirituality and mystery are always difficult to put into words.

The spiritual muscle of character, endurance, courage, and hope, which we develop in this wilderness, will carry us through. It will carry us through when life's deserts come again. It will carry us through to new joys.

If you have been through grief, you understand that sadness and depression are often experienced as loneliness. You know it takes time and work to get through it. You know the road is not easy. As with the caterpillar, you know that in order to become a butterfly, a transformed creation, you must enter a process of giving up the way life has been in order to find new life. You know that metamorphosis is difficult work but brings transformation.

When Depression is Too Deep and Dark, Get Help!

As positive as I am about the importance of sadness and depression in healing, there are danger signs to watch for in complicated and deep depression. These are the signs which point to when grief's normal sadness and depression moves into what is called clinical depression. Clinical depression can lead to dysfunction, illness, suicidal thoughts and, on rare occasions, attempts at suicide. When the grieving person gets to this level of suffering, he or she needs to get help.

As positive as I am about the importance of sadness and depression in healing, there are danger signs to watch for in complicated and deep depression.

SIGNS OF WHEN DEPRESSION IS TOO DEEP

The following are five symptoms to look for in depression. They can be warning signs that we need more help to make it through the wilderness of grief. Remember that some levels of each of these signs or symptoms are also present in normal grief work. I have tried to describe them in the previous paragraphs and chapters. But in some situations, our past experiences of separation anxiety, dependency, losses, fear, or hopelessness may surface in the present grief experience. This can happen without our even knowing.

Clinical depression may also be experienced when our grief is complicated. Complicated grief has a number of causes. It may be when we are dealing with more than one loss or death at the same time. Examples of this may be the loss of a parent and a spouse in the same two-year period. The death of a child can erupt major bouts of depression. The death of a spouse may resurface grief or abandonment issues of long ago when our parent died or perhaps went through divorce.

Our past experiences of separation anxiety, dependency, loss, fear, or hopelessness may surface in the present grief experience. This can happen without our even knowing.

---

1. *Dramatic and unusual changes in appetite* leading to significant weight loss or gain over a six-month period or less, is the first symptom to watch for. In normal grief reaction and healing processes it is quite normal to overeat or undereat in the midst of pain and loneliness. As infants we cried out for comfort and

were often given milk of the breast or bottle to satisfy and comfort us. The same is true for the child still in all of us. We may overeat in search of comfort or we may undereat because of no appetite. When this goes on for a lengthy time and a large percentage of weight loss or gain is the result, then this may be one of the signs of clinical depression and not just a normal grief reaction. We need to watch this closely, because ongoing dramatic changes in body weight can also affect our immune system and invite illnesses. Help may be needed beyond good grieving.

2. *Dramatic and unusual changes in sleep patterns* are common in grief. The following are examples. We go to bed at the normal time and we toss and turn and cannot fall asleep until 4:00 a.m. We are supposed to be up at 6:00 to go to work. Or we are able to go to sleep immediately when our head hits the pillow, but we wake at 2:00 and cannot go back to sleep for hours. Or we sleep all the time and cannot get out of bed or get to work. Sleep pattern changes take many forms. Remember, it is common to have sleep pattern changes in the midst of normal grief adjustment. The problems begin when these symptoms keep on for long periods of time and begin to affect our health, work, or relationships. Not getting good sound rest can also contribute to higher levels of anxiety and sadness. Help may be needed beyond good grieving.

3. *Dramatic and unusual changes in sexual appetite or other behavior* are common in grief. Clinical depression can sometimes be identified by one's lack of interest in sex or inability to perform sexually. Grief often drains the bottom out of our sexual interest. On the other hand, in grief sexual needs may increase. The need for sexual closeness may become a search for comfort in the midst of pain and loneliness. In depression and loneliness, some who have lost a partner may participate in sexual behaviors that are beyond their former values. If you have lost a love partner to death or divorce, you may already be facing and dealing with these changes. If sexual dysfunction or lack of interest continues for long periods of time, then you may be suffering from clinical depression beyond a normal grief reaction. Help may be needed beyond good grieving.

4. *Lack of motivation and interest in everyday work or activities, often accompanied by fatigue,* is a common experience in grief.

Bouts of fatigue and lack of interest or motivation are quite normal. But, if these symptoms go on for long periods of time, they can lead to other dysfunctions, such as inadequate functioning at home and at work. This can develop to the point of interrupting one's career or one's responsibilities as caregiver to children. Help may be needed beyond good grieving.

5. *Suicidal ideations or specific suicide plans* may interrupt everyday thoughts. Suicidal ideations are any thoughts of hurting oneself or taking one's life. If we, or someone we love, are experiencing or expressing thoughts of hopelessness, especially if these thoughts are associated with suicidal thoughts, *get the person or yourself to professional help immediately.* Sometimes persons who have lost a spouse or someone dear to them, may verbalize hopelessness such as, "I just don't have anything to live for anymore." This may or may not be suicidal ideation. Keep listening and ask some questions for clarification

Six months after my mother's sudden death, Dad and I were driving down the road talking about her. He said, "I just don't have anything to live for now that Mom is gone. The house gets pretty lonely."

I wondered to myself if this suicidal thinking or natural grieving. I explored it with him more closely and asked, "Dad, do you think about that a lot?"

Dad replied, "Every day I miss her and I wonder what there is to live for anymore."

I then asked, "Dad, let me ask about this. Are you having any thoughts of ending your life or hurting yourself?"

To my relief he responded, "No, son, I couldn't do anything like that. It's just that it gets so lonely without her."

My father's expressed feelings and thoughts were a part of normal grief and adjustment that any companion may go through. But if he had said, "Well, I keep having thoughts about all that medication in the medicine cabinet." Or if he had responded, "I drive down the freeway and just want to run off the road and kill myself. I don't want to do it. I don't believe in it, but the thoughts won't go away." If this were what he or anyone would have said, I would have insisted that he get professional care, including medical assessment for depression.

GETTING HELP: WHEN, WHAT, AND WHERE

This last symptom of suicidal ideation is quite serious. We can pray for, counsel, and listen to someone who is severely depressed and the person may be dead by morning if we missed the suicidal symptoms. Without medications and counseling the person in this severe state of depression may not be able to go into the wilderness or do grief work in a healthy way until he or she has had medical help and professional counseling. Don't take that chance with yourself or with someone you love. If clinical depression is present, get help!

Without medications and counseling, the person in a severe state of depression may not be able to go into the desert and do grief work in a healthy way.

How do you know when someone needs help? Does it take one, two, three, or all of the previous symptoms before getting help? How do you assess yourself? My experience is that as you read this list you will know whether you need professional help. But at times it can be difficult to know for certain or to take the first step toward help. If your suffering is to the point that your functioning is impaired for a considerable period of time, go to a clinically trained clergy, physician, psychiatrist, therapist or counselor, social worker, or other mental health care professional and talk it over with him or her. These are professionals who should be able to help you or refer you to someone who specializes in grief.

What Kind of Help Do I Need?

Certainly therapy and coaching are beneficial to anyone who grieves, whether clinically depressed or not. By talking out our feelings and thoughts we adjust more quickly and healthfully. This can be with your pastor if you sense he or she is a person who cares deeply and listens empathically. If your pastor explains your depression as lack of faith, go talk to someone else.

Once you explore this with a professional you may discover that medications are needed to help you through the wilderness of grief. Usually these are antidepressants, which may have helpful effects when suffering is deep and continuous. Keep your doctor informed as to side effects and effectiveness of the medication. Many types of effective antidepressant drugs are on the market and each person's chemistry responds differently to each medication.

Once you start taking your medication, you should notice in two to five weeks that you are starting to sleep better. After a month or so, you should begin to have more energy, feel less worried and anxious, and have fewer and hopefully no thoughts of suicide. Please understand that the goal of medication is not to take all your pain and grief away. The goal of medication is to relieve the deep, deep suffering and darkness so that you can mourn and grieve in a helpful and healthy way.

Depression is an unwanted gift, but it is a gift. It is a gift of the spiritual/ emotional self which often cannot be understood by the rational self.

Depression is an unwanted gift. It is a gift of the spiritual/emotional self which often cannot be understood by the rational self. Depression and sadness usually express the meaning and value we place on the connection, bond and love we experience with the one who is now not with us. Your depression may be expressing gratitude for this special relationship. We do not become deeply saddened or depressed over those with whom we have had little involvement.

With each journey into the darkness, the darkness has less control. The healing light is coming through the darkness to meet us.

In the healing journey through the wilderness, sadness or depression may often return. But when we have the courage to feel it, follow it, walk into it, wrestle it, and search it, the darkness of depression approaches more and more light. With each journey into the darkness, the darkness has less control because light is coming through the darkness to meet us.

Chapter 8

Healing:
Experiencing the Light Again

The wilderness does lead to a promised life. Grief faithfully unwraps the dawn. The sun does come up again or perhaps we notice that the sun is coming up again. The darkness has let go to light and healing.

Susan was a recently widowed, young pregnant mother with a two-year-old son, and she entered grief counseling just after her daughter was born. Her husband's tragic death was a tremendous blow to her life, love, and dreams.

The wilderness does lead to a promised life. Grief faithfully unwraps the dawn.

Each week she talked through the loss, sadness, confusion, loneliness, abandonment, disbelief, and frustration regarding James's death. She wrestled in the wilderness of widowhood and single parenting. Each week she told her story, processing thoughts and feelings over and over again. Many times I knew what she was going to say before she said it because she had expressed her pain over and over so many times.

After many months, there were new themes in her grief story. She was shaping a future story. Susan began to talk more about the children's growth rather than focusing primarily on loss and confusion. However, after each new movement forward, she circled back to her husband's death. She wrestled with the "why" question that is often asked after death. Susan wrestled with the sadness that her children would never see their father again.

The Unwanted Gift of Grief: A Ministry Approach
© 2006 by The Haworth Press, Inc. All rights reserved.
doi:10.1300/5644_09

With each passing month her thoughts became more focused on the children's growth, new friends, a new job, and new dating experiences. She began to talk about the present and the future more than loss in the past. Susan was moving toward the light.

TURNING POINTS IN THE WILDERNESS

On one occasion, Susan interrupted herself in the middle of a session and said, "It seems like I say the same things every week. Don't you get bored hearing this?" Her question demonstrated what I call a turning point. Not a sudden turning point, but a subtle turning point that slowly takes form in grief work. I was not bored because over the previous months I could detect in her stories the latent transformation of themes, emotions, voice, and hopefulness. What was significant was that now Susan recognized that she was moving into the light again. She recognized that she was in transformation and healing.

Susan faithfully moved through the darkness and out of the intensity of grief. Soon after this, she decided she would not need grief counseling regularly and asked if she could call for an appointment as needed. She had survived and knew that transformation was taking place in her life. I could see it. She could feel it. She was beginning to experience differentiation from the past and her deceased husband. Susan's growing autonomy was taking on the promise of a new story, life, hope, and resurrection.

Acceptance and healing are not the same.

Acceptance and healing are different. In acceptance one experiences the light again, but the anxieties, fears, and sadness are still profoundly present. They are still present but manageable. In acceptance, the sadness and depression lift considerably, yet at times they dance their way back into our path.

In acceptance one experiences the light again, but the anxieties, fears, and sadness are still profoundly present. They are present but manageable.

Notice that Susan still wanted to be sure I would see her if she needed. That's the nature of acceptance and early light. We courageously venture out but also move cautiously and slowly. When first walking on a leg after it has been broken, we tend to walk slowly and at first we do not put all our weight on it. It has to be strengthened and rehabilitated. However, enough healing may be present so that we can trust to walk on it.

Grief heals similarly. First, we come to accept loss and slowly come to believe that somehow we will make it. In the dawn of healing, we are slow to walk again, for our wounded soul does not yet feel ready to take on the full weight of life and love. So at times we crawl.

We courageously venture out but move cautiously and slowly.

Not everything in life reminds us of loss.

In acceptance, not everything in life reminds us of our loss. Dwelling and obsession on the past dissipates. We can think about other things and take on new interests, friends, and activities. We are not completely free from emotional pain, but free enough to take on some new choices and set new goals.

We are not completely free from emotional pain, but free enough to take on some new choices and set new goals.

We may notice an intermittent soft sense of guilt or fear because we fear that healing means we are leaving our loved one behind to the past. On the contrary, healing means we are taking his or her love and memories into the future with us. Grief may have been one of the ways that we stay connected to our deceased child or spouse and now we are letting our grief go. Our sense of guilt or fear may cause us to ask, "Does this also mean that I am letting my loved one go? Does this mean I will forget him or her?" This can intensify our pain momentarily because we do not want to let our loved one go, and grief was one of the ways we may have stayed connected with him or her.

We may notice an intermittent soft sense of guilt or fear because we fear that healing means we are leaving our loved one behind to the past. On the contrary, healing means we are taking his or her love and memories into the future with us.

As we first move into the light, we may feel driven to make it through, start over, or to change our life. In this way, acceptance of a loss and healing through a loss are two different experiences on the journey. In acceptance we may still have a tendency to push ourselves and feel driven to "make it," while in a healing state we begin to experience life as gift and an invitation to live again.

In acceptance we may still have a tendency to push ourselves and feel driven to "make it," while in a healing state we begin to experience life as gift and an invitation again.

For example, in acceptance the new widower may come to the middle of the week and realize he has no plans for the weekend. Not wanting to feel the pain of being alone, he may get on the phone and anxiously set up activities with friends. Initiating activities with friends is important, but sometimes we keep ourselves overly busy in order not to feel the grief now. In acceptance, we know the cards that are on the table of life and we know we must use them. We may realize that money is short and now we are the only income producer. As a result, we go out and find a job or a better paying job. We do this not because we *want* to, but because we *have* to in order to make it. Perhaps we go back to school to get another degree in order to enhance the income. Perhaps we move into the kitchen and force ourselves to learn to cook. We may even make ourselves go out on dates. We go, not so much because we enjoy it, but because we don't want to be alone.

CAUTION: EUPHORIA MAY BE AHEAD!

Times of euphoria are common in the early stages of acceptance and healing. It feels so good to feel like ourself again. Enjoy the euphoria but for a while don't trust it as the final word. Take it slow.

Euphoria may be out ahead. Enjoy the euphoria but for a while don't trust it as the final word. Take it slow.

Our endorphins and adrenaline are pumping again. Perhaps even our hormones are alive again. This can be a fun time. We deserve it after wrestling so long through the dark wilderness. CAUTION! The decisions made during this period of euphoria are not always the best decisions.

CAUTION! We may not yet be ready to trust all of our decisions and wishes. For example, exhilarating experiences of romantic attachment may cause us to make permanent commitments or marriage decisions too early. We may misjudge a transitional relationship, mistaking it for a permanent relationship. If this is the case, we may have jumped out of the hot skillet of grief into the fire of euphoric short-sightedness. Take things easy for awhile. Don't trust euphoria as the decisive emotion. Life and love does include peak experiences, but real and lasting relationships also have struggles. If you fall in love during this stage of the healing journey, try to wear out the relationship for a couple of years and see if you continue to be good for each other over the long haul of life.

CAUTION! The decisions made during this period of euphoria are not always the best decisions. During this period we may want to delay major decisions as much as possible.

During this period we may want to delay major decisions as much as possible. Perhaps we need to hold off until some of the euphoria dissipates. Do not be blinded by the light, just enjoy it. This is a time that you want to move slowly and wisely. Enjoy your changing self and get some more healing under your belt.

Almost, but not yet! The surge of energy that comes after the wrestle in the wilderness is a breath of fresh air. There are moments of feeling wonderful, as if we are a new being. Yet, there are intermittent times of sadness and regrieving. During this period we may come home from dates and realize that during the entire date we were comparing the data with our deceased love. We may come home from these dates and feel like crying and don't know why.

There are moments of feeling wonderful as if we are a new being. Yet there are intermittent times of sadness and regrieving.

WHAT DOES THIS HEALING TRANSFORMATION LOOK OR FEEL LIKE?

Healing means life feels like an invitation again.

Healing means life feels like an invitation again. Healing is what the unwanted gift of grief is moving us toward. We only get to healthy healing by going through the wilderness and developing the spiritual muscles and inner resources that grief can teach us. Healing feels as if life is inviting us to live again. Life becomes an invitation without the anxious drivenness in the wilderness.

Differentiating is part of the transforming processes of growing up. This process is busy and profound in childhood and adolescence but also continues throughout our adult lives. As children differentiate and individuate from parents they leave them and cleave to new life and love. In the grief process, we differentiate and individuate from our past love in order to take his or her love and spirit with us and create a new life and love in the future.

In the grief process, we differentiate and individuate from our past love in order to take his or her love and spirit with us and create a new life and love in the future.

Differentiation is at the heart of healthy relationships. Differentiation means that I am me and you are you. Yes, we mutually share and dream together. Yes, we love each other and tackle life together. However, differentiation and individuation means that we don't worship each other. We are not so connected together that we become enmeshed, or as a more popular term puts it, "codependent" upon each other. In codependent relationships, we lose our separate identities. In healthy relationships, both persons stand before God as separate beings and enflesh God's love to each other as separate beings. Constantly we are working in love to make two one, while never losing our separate identities. We have commitment and love, but do not lose our identities in one another while creating a mission together.

What does all of this have to do with healing? Healing means coming to the relaxed awareness that we are *in* the world but not *of* the world. We are *in* the relationship but not *of* the relationship.

What does all of this have to do with healing? Healing means coming to the relaxed awareness that we are in *the world but not* of *the world. We are* in *the relationship but not* of *the relationship.*

We do mourn deeply the loss of our togetherness, but we slowly learn that our togetherness is not all there is to life. We discover that we can risk the pain to love and live again.

Healing does not mean leaving our loved one behind.

The hope of effective parenting is to love our children and slowly give them to themselves and the world. The hope is that as the child grows and leaves the parents, the child will internalize the parents' love and take it with him or her into successful living as a unique and separate person. This internalization process is similar when we lose a loved one in death. We do not leave the person behind. Instead we celebrate his or her life and love by taking his or her love with us into the future. With this love internalized within us, we go on to love others more effectively and joyfully. We love our living children better because we internalize the love of our deceased child. We love in new relationships better because we internalize the love of our past love.

With this love internalized within us, we go on to love others more effectively and joyfully.

When Derrick remarried five years after his wife died of cancer, he constantly compared his new wife to his first. He could not seem to accept and enjoy his new wife just as she was. This illustrates that Derrick had not healed but only accepted his previous wife's death. Over the years, his new wife began to feel unloved and not accepted for her unique self. Derrick had not differentiated. He had not internalized his first wife's love and had not moved on to love his new wife more fully because of his memories of the past. He was stuck. Derrick had some grief work yet to do.

Derrick was stuck in the glorification of his first wife. For awhile glorification is quite common in grief. Glorifying or edifying the person into perfection and near sainthood is common. The truth is that the person was human and had clay feet and weaknesses just as we all have clay feet and weaknesses.

Healing means living life to the fullest, because of our memories.

The hope of healing is to live life to the fullest because of our memories of love. We need not live life in eternal mourning, as if, our mourning were a memorial to him or her. We need to live more fully, lovingly, and joyfully because of our memories of the person. This fullness of life becomes a memorial to our past love.

We need not live life in eternal mourning as if our mourning were a memorial to him or her. We need to live more fully, lovingly, and joyfully because of our memories of the person. This fullness of life becomes a memorial to our past love.

The way we make this transformation is through the wilderness of grief. The way we come to this light is through the darkness. The way we heal is through the labor and contractions of leaving the old and coming into the light of new life and love. We must die to the old and rise up to new life. Said simply but mysteriously, we internalize the lost loved one's spirit within our spirit, and God's Spirit invites us into the future.

We need sojourners and support in the wilderness.

We need sojourners to walk with us through the wilderness. In the wilderness of grief, it is common that hurting people develop a sorority or fraternity of friends and fellow strugglers who will go through the wilderness together. Perhaps we meet at singles groups, widows and widowers support group, or just happened to be introduced. Perhaps we meet another couple with a mentally retarded child. Perhaps we meet another couple that lost a baby. These friends come together through a common denominator called grief and loss and support each other. These individuals and groups often cut across social, economic, faith, and cultural barriers. Differences and prejudice often turn into empathy and compassion after people know suffering as a common denominator. These individuals may become our community for awhile or for a lifetime.

In the wilderness of grief, it is common that hurting people develop a sorority or fraternity of friends and fellow strugglers who will go through the wilderness together.

As we heal we may notice that we don't spend as much time with this support community. It's similar to graduating from high school or college and losing touch. This is a common experience in the healing process. The pull of pain that kept us together, supporting each other in the past, isn't as strong now. We are transforming and going on from our grief, grief partners, and sojourners. Now life has new transcending pulls. Our new life brings new community, but we will forever remember in our hearts these fellow strugglers in the wilderness. We have internalized their love also. Talk openly with them regarding these transitions. This becomes an opportunity to express gratitude to one another for sharing the wilderness together.

As we heal we may notice that we don't spend as much time with this support community. Life has new transcending pulls now. Our new life brings new community, but we will forever remember these fellow strugglers.

Jeanne and I have been married more than twenty years. She was widowed in her mid-twenties. On her fiftieth birthday, I pulled off a surprise birthday party for her. She could not believe that I pulled it off, nor could I. Seventy friends and family members attended from across the United States. In developing the invitation list and calling people, I realized the many communities, sororities, and sojourners in her life. Many family members of her deceased husband came to the party. Some, she had not seen in years. Nine-month-old Tommy flew in from the East coast with April, his mother. April was Jeanne's deceased husband's younger sister. Little Tommy was named after him. Jeanne cried as she held the little fellow.

A widow friend was also present. The two had shared the wilderness together in their single-again days. They laughed and reminisced about their days of singlehood as if it was just the week before rather than almost three decades ago. It was a night of history, tears, laughter, and celebration. I loved it. Jeanne loved it. This night made me aware of how we heal through grief and come to experience life as invitation again. We move through the unwanted gift of grief and, if we are faithful to the gift, life becomes a new creation.

We move through the unwanted gift of grief and, if we are faithful to the gift, life becomes a new creation.

What does it look or feel like to be in the light again? Everyone experiences this transformation differently, but let me go back to an earlier illustration to clarify. In healing you may experience something similar to the following. You're single again and you realize in the middle of the week that you don't have any plans for the weekend. In a relaxed way you think through your options and all the activities you could plan or structure. "Well, I could call Joey or Evelyn and see what they are up to . . . or I could go to a movie . . . or I could just curl up in front of the fireplace and read my book."

In healing, the person has entered or returned to a state of being emotionally and spiritually full rather than emotionally and spiritually hungry or empty. In this relaxed peaceful state, it doesn't really matter which options this single-again person chooses. What matters is that there is peace. He or she has healed through the anxiety and grief that previously hit when he or she was alone. Life has come to be *invitation* again, rather than feeling *driven* or pushed to plan something in order to avoid the grief. In healing we can talk about our loss or not talk about our loss without having our throat tightened by tears and emotions. It is as if God is in the present with us, not just in the past, and not just in the future.

In healing the person has returned to a state of being emotionally and spiritually full rather than emotionally and spiritually hungry or empty.

Healing means deeper wisdom, humor, and spirituality.

In healing we develop deep wisdom, humor, and spirituality. These are spiritual muscles that are developed while in the grief wilderness. Wisdom is the capacity to see through things as they are and live through them. Humor is the capacity to see through things as they are and laugh through them. Spirituality is the capacity to see through things as they are and hope through them.

Wisdom is the capacity to see through things as they are and live through them. Humor is the capacity to see through things as they are and laugh through them. Spirituality is the capacity to see through things as they are and hope through them.

The hope of the wilderness of grief is the capacity to see through things as they are and heal through them. In other words, it is the capacity to live faithfully this side of mystery. Healing is the capacity to live with mystery while still not fully understanding.

The hope of the wilderness of grief is that we develop the capacity to live faithfully this side of mystery. Healing is the capacity to live with mystery while still not fully understanding.

Grief as the Unwanted Gift.

All along in the wilderness, we knew but we could not see. The pain was blinding. We slowly came to see that our grief was our gratitude. Our gratitude for our lost loved one. We had a bond with him or her. He or she mattered to us. We were involved with the person. We loved him or her and he or she loved us. We do not grieve significantly over those with whom we had no bond or love.

As our grief transforms into healing, I hope we take time to sit and remember and mourn over our deceased partner or child. But remember, remember that our tears are our gratitude rather than just our grasping. Our tears are celebrating love. We only grieve over those we love. Forever, we can celebrate their gift of love. Imperfect love? Yes. He or she made human mistakes and we made human mistakes. But most of all, love!

Remember that our tears are our gratitude rather than just our grasping. Our tears are celebrating love. We only grieve over those we love. Forever, we can celebrate their gift of love.

WHAT IS THIS MYSTERIOUS SPIRIT THAT TRANSFORMS US THROUGH THE WILDERNESS?

What is it that moves us through the wilderness of grief? First, we must have the courage to use the vehicles of grief. Grief was given to us by our Creator to help us wrestle our way through our crosses to healing and resurrection. Grief and grief work are gifts to be used rather than avoided.

Yet, still it is a mystery to me as to how and why we get through the wilderness. Many times I encounter people who have lost so much and hurt so deeply that I wondered to myself, "Will they ever feel the light again? Will they ever be able to go on with life again?" Then to my joyful surprise, they mysteriously healed and transformed through the wilderness.

First, we must have the courage to use the vehicles of grief. It was given by our Creator to help us wrestle our way through our crosses to healing and resurrection. Grief and grief work are gifts to be used rather than avoided.

It must be mystery! It must be the mysterious Spirit of God who heals us and brings us to transformation and new life. This Divine Creator, Comforter, Sustainer, and Redeemer weeps with us when we hurt, but never grows faint or weary. This is the one who walks with us through the wilderness and toward the light. This Holy One was the light all along, but we could not see beyond our pain. This ever-present one never faints or grows weary! As a result, we become people of hope again!

This Divine Creator, Comforter, Sustainer, and Redeemer weeps with us when we hurt, but never grows faint or weary. This Holy One was the light all along, but we could not see beyond our pain. This ever-present one never faints or grows weary! As a result, we become a people of hope again!

Have you not known? Have you not heard?
The Lord is the everlasting God,
the Creator of the ends of the earth.
He does not faint or grow weary,
His understanding is unsearchable.
He gives power to the faint,
and to him (or her) who has no might he increases strength.
Even youths shall faint and be weary,
and young men (and women) shall fall exhausted;
but they who wait for the Lord shall renew their strength,
they shall mount up with wings like eagles,
they shall run and not be weary,
they shall walk and not faint.

Isaiah 40:28-31 RSV (parentheses mine)

Chapter 9

And Yet . . . We Never Forget!

THE RETURN OF GRIEF:
"PEEK-A-BOO" EXPERIENCES

And yet, even after healing and light finally arrive and we have moved on with our lives, the light still is interrupted by occasional shadows. These shadows surface when memories of our loss or lost love peek through our busy minds. We are often surprised by the emotions that return, although now they usually are not as powerful. I call these "peek-a-boo" grief experiences because they seem to peek out and startle us when we least expect them. Sometimes the experiences that vibrate these emotions are so subtle we may not be aware of why we feel the way we do until hours or days later.

Even after healing we are often surprised by the emotions that occasionally return, although usually they are not as powerful. I call these "peek-a-boo" grief experiences because they seem to peek out and startle us when we least expect them.

Years after Abby's birth my tears frequently grabbed me by surprise and would not let me go. On one of these occasions, I was glad I was hidden behind a camera taking pictures. At age eight, children with mental and physical handicaps are eligible to participate in the Special Olympics. This particular experience took place when Abby was eight. It was her first year to participate in "The Games."

When we arrived at the stadium I noticed a sad shadow gathering in me and over me, but was not sure from where it was coming. Was it seeing my daughter with all the other kids with handicaps? Was it pride

The Unwanted Gift of Grief: A Ministry Approach
© 2006 by The Haworth Press, Inc. All rights reserved.
doi:10.1300/5644_10

because she had prepared for weeks for her race in the fifty-yard dash and relay team? Or was it just a tough day?

At the opening ceremonies of every Special Olympic event, the torch is carried around the stadium by special olympians. Usually a local law enforcement officer or dignitary runs with each of the four olympians as they carry the torch together. I did not know until moments before the opening ceremonies that Abby had been selected as one of the four athletes to run the torch around the stadium. I was a proud father. I was behind my camera ready to capture the moment the torch was passed to Abby. The moment came and I came apart. As she ran with the torch, every emotion imaginable also ran through me. I could not stop crying, so I just stayed behind my camera after the run was over.

These were not just tears of a proud father touched by his beautiful daughter's valiant efforts, although I was a proud father. These tears connected back to eight years before when she was born. That night I was struck with shock and sadness. That was the night when our pediatrician said the words "your daughter has Down syndrome." The tears were profound. Although I knew I was feeling strange on the opening day of Abby's first Special Olympics, I had no idea the volume of grief that needed to be expressed. Earlier I had concluded I was just a proud father.

And yet! Even after years of healing, there are still times of shadows and momentary grief for most people. These are shadows of sadness, disbelief, frustration, anger, hurt, or abandonment. The list goes on. These peek-a-boo feelings are usually engaged by an event, memory, or perhaps they are feelings that have collected little by little until the bucket of grief within us is filled and needs emptying.

These peek-a-boo feelings are usually engaged by an event or memory or perhaps they are feelings that have collected little by little until the bucket of grief within us is filled and needs emptying.

Recently a colleague of mine became a grandmother for the second time. Jane was widowed five years before. After her daughter gave birth to a perfect grandchild, Jane felt down, discouraged, and sad for a number of days. She did not have much energy or interest in anything. Jane felt a little guilty that she was not celebrating the excitement of her new grandchild. Days later, Jane's subliminal grief moved powerfully into full consciousness and awareness. She awoke in tears in the middle of the night. The tears were connected to the thoughts of her deceased husband and the grandfather of this beautiful baby. Henry was dead and would never see his grandchild nor would his grandchild experience him.

For a number of hours that night Jane wept the emotions that had been gathering without her full awareness. It was like a hurricane slowly gathering force before hitting the shore. The next morning she felt lighter, energized, and motivated. Happiness had returned. She shared her experience with her daughter the next day. The daughter also had collected a ton of tears. The daughter had also been feeling moody and sad when she felt she should be enjoying her new baby. Sharing her story of the previous night, the mother helped her daughter process the grief which each of them had thought was over and healed.

Grief can gather like a teapot on the stove. In the teapot, the water converts into steam and at some point signals readiness to the chef. In grief, the pain is there but it is so subtle that we put it away in the teapot within us. We think we have forgotten it and moved on with life. Then another event reminds us of the loss. It may be the time of the year, a special night, certain music, a crying baby, a date, or seeing someone at the mall who reminded us of the lost love. The grief teapot gathers steam slowly and often without our knowing. And then suddenly it whistles and reminds us to deal with our built-up grief and emotions.

We think we have forgotten grief and moved on with life. Then another event reminds us of the loss. It may be the time of the year, a special night, certain music, a crying baby, a date, or seeing someone at the mall who reminded us of the lost love.

Many people are not aware of grief shadows or the subtle gathering emotions. Therefore, they may not allow it to be expressed, experienced, and released. This release and expression is known as catharsis. Spiritually, I call it confession. Some try to avoid it and swallow the grief a little harder and, as a result, may find themselves frustrated, impatient with others, or even unable to concentrate. We must honor our grief and let it have its say. When we do not permit our grief its expression, life itself can begin to lose its delight.

We must honor our grief and let it have its say. When we do not permit our grief its expression, life itself can begin to lose its delight.

Our memories are gifts. Yes, we go on with life. We marry again or have another baby. We do heal. The light does find us in the dark wilderness and leads us into God's promised land and life. In spite of the fact that we are happy and life is good again, life also engages our memories and grief shadows may return. Grief is gratitude and we only grieve because we valued and cherished the one we lost. He or she had a meaningful place in our lives. Grief is an unwanted gift, but a gift. We need to embrace it and work it through. Each unfolding emotion and each unfolding shadow is an opportunity to value life as it has been and transforms life into the way it can be.

Grief is an unwanted gift, but a gift. We need to embrace it and work it through. Each unfolding emotion and each unfolding shadow is an opportunity to value life as it has been and transform life into the way it can be.

This was just a routine visit from the hospital chaplain. I wanted to go by and offer congratulations and celebrate with Donna and John the birth of their healthy, bouncing baby boy. I had not known them before. As we visited, I began to realize how important my visit was and how grateful they were for the chance to tell their story. As they cried and talked, I listened.

Almost five years before they had lost a three-year-old son. They loved and enjoyed Michael every day of his short life. Mysteriously he had entered a neighbor's backyard gate and had drowned in the swimming pool. They told me of the wrenching months and years after that. At times they wondered if their marriage would make it. Even trying to be intimate seemed to bring such profound emotional pain that for a long while they avoided one another sexually.

Into the second year after Michael's death, they realized that not only had they lost a child, but also they were losing each other. Their marriage was falling apart. Each of them avoided the other. Also, they did not trust themselves to care for another baby. They were not sure they could love and risk losing another child.

They entered marriage therapy and participated in grief counseling and coaching. They learned to cry openly with each other, learned not to avoid talking about Michael, and more important, they learned to rekindle their love for each other.

After some hard work and hard grieving in therapy, they began to risk new life together. As I listened to their story in that hospital room with their new baby, Jessica, in the bassinet beside them, I was touched. I was listening to a young couple that had courage amidst fear, had faith amidst doubt, and had hope amidst despair.

Donna and John had used the unwanted gift of grief for healing. This couple knew that crossing the wilderness was a wrestle, but they courageously crossed the wilderness. They learned to face the "and yet" of life. They loved again and risked love again. They chose to say "yes" to the future and carry the past shadows of pain and joy with them, as they loved each other and their new baby more deeply in the present.

Life moves on, and yet we never forget the loss of the one we love. We remember and feel gratitude in the midst of our pain.

People around us may not understand the grief that shows up years later. There are some things others cannot understand nor will they ever understand until some dramatic loss disturbs their lives. It seems that life's wounds become our great teachers of empathy and then we can become "wounded healers" for others.

Move at your own pace not other's expectations. Yet, at the same time, continue to move toward light and new life. Move away from worshipping the past but honor the past. Love life and others more because of the past.

Move at your own pace, not according to other's expectations. Yet, at the same time, continue to move toward light and new life. Move away from worshiping the past, but honor the past. Love life and others more because of the past. Let the shadows be with you. God is the God of our past. God is the God of our present. God is the God of our future. And God is also the God of the unwanted gift of grief through the wilderness. This sustaining one calls you into the future. Say "yes" to that call.

PART III:
SOJOURNERS IN THE WILDERNESS—
HOW TO HELP

Chapter 10

Being a Sojourner

When a loved one or part of life is lost, one often feels devastated and alone. The grieving person needs support from one who listens and tries to understand. I call this person a sojourner. Over the years, I have often noticed that family members, friends, congregation members, work associates, and even health care professionals and clergy avoid the person who is in the throes of intense grief. I do not believe they avoid them because these individuals lack concern, but because they do not know what to say. Usually, they care deeply but do not know how to communicate care. In the awkwardness, they often say little, change the subject, or make positive comments in hopes of making the hurting person feel better.

The suggestions and guidelines ahead are offered to help the professional or layperson be a more effective sojourners with those who grieve. These suggestions are not meant to be exhaustive, but brief and concise coaching. These principles and practices are drawn from my ministry and seminars at the Memorial Hermann Healthcare System. The following comments will be better understood after reading the previous chapters.

WHAT IS A SOJOURNER?

A sojourner is one who intentionally supports a grieving person through the wilderness of grief. This may be a friend, family member, colleague, chaplain, minister, priest, rabbi, social worker, counselor, therapist, nurse, physician, or other health care professional. The

The Unwanted Gift of Grief: A Ministry Approach
© 2006 by The Haworth Press, Inc. All rights reserved.
doi:10.1300/5644_11

sojourner dwells and journeys with the grieving person. Unfortunately, sojourners are few in number. If you find one, you have found
a treasure.

Sojourners are people with empathy. Empathy is the capacity to
enter another person's frame of reference, perspective, thoughts, feelings, and grief, as if it were one's own. However, sojourners never
lose their own perspective. These empathic persons can be with others in pain without trying to take their pain away. The sojourner emp-
ties out of her or his self in order to enter another's world and walk in
another person's shoes.

Sojourners know how to listen and take time to listen. They know
how to love but not love too much. They know how to "incarnate
love," which is to put into flesh God's love for the other, yet they
know they are not God. They know that God's spirit heals the person
as the sojourner listens and supports with time, mercy, and grace.
This is incarnate love. This is sojourning.

---

*The sojourner empathically listens and dwells with, walks with, cries with,
and laughs with the person in the grief wilderness. The sojourner knows
that the human spirit and God's spirit will heal in time, but also knows that
healing is more effective and less lonely when support is available. The sojourner knows the "way" is difficult and filled with varied emotions.*

Sojourners know that people do not all grieve the same or unfold in
predictable pathways. Grief does not follow exact stages or phases. In
fact, the grieving person may be in a different place each time we visit
with him or her. The sojourner needs a "microscopic" listening ability. Microscopic listening is the ability to focus one's eyes, ears, mind,
and heart on the emotions, thoughts, or actions that the grieving person is experiencing today and in this moment. If the sojourner attempts
to put the person in an expected pathway, phase or stage, we run the
risk of not understanding the person and his or her not feeling understood.

Carl Rogers names basic empathic listening—being with and understanding—as an "unappreciated way of being."[1] Rogers defines
basic empathic listening, or "being with," as follows:

It means entering the private perceptual world of the other and becoming thoroughly at home in it. It involves being sensitive, moment by moment, to the changing felt meanings which flow in this other person, to the fear or rage or tenderness or confusion or whatever that he or she is experiencing. It means temporarily living in the other's life, moving about in it delicately without making judgments.[2]

The sojourner may meet with a person one time but usually sojourning is an ongoing commitment, ranging from a couple of sessions to regular sessions either daily, weekly, or monthly. So much depends on the needs of the grieving person. The following are designed to help us all be more sensitive and effective caregivers with those who are crossing the wilderness of grief.

Characteristics of a Sojourner

Sojourners . . .

- are people of love and communicate love;
- make time for others but also make time for themselves;
- keep caring, yet know they may not care perfectly;
- listen, and listen, and listen;
- do not talk others out of their grief, but help others talk out their grief;
- know that everyone grieves differently;
- can be present amidst another's painful emotions;
- invite others to say more about feelings, such as: fear, anger, depression, sadness, anxiety, disbelief, denial, joy, or euphoria;
- value the story of another human being;
- often have personally experienced grief and, as a result, are more compassionate;
- often become wounded healers;
- do not give easy answers;
- do not say, "I understand," but say, "I don't understand. Tell me and help me understand"; and
- rarely share their own story of pain and, if they do, are careful not to let the conversation focus on them.

APPENDIX: THE SOJOURNER PROCESS GUIDE—
WALKING WITH ANOTHER THROUGH
THE WILDERNESS OF GRIEF

The following is a seventeen-step process used by the sojourner and the grieving person during their grief sessions together. Copy these guidelines and take them with you to the session. It might also be helpful to give copies to family and friends of the grieving person. They could benefit from understanding these helping principles.

If you are married or close family members grieving the same loss, use the "grief date" guidelines at the end of Chapter 16 titled, "Marriage: Tough Enough Without Grief." These guidelines need to be copied and be available during times together. You will find a copy in the appendix. It is difficult and challenging to listen and support each other well. These guidelines are offered as help.

The chapters after these guidelines include more specific suggestions for helping people in darkness, frustration, anger, praying for a miracle, sadness, depression, healing, and marriage. Please read these chapters in conjunction with the corresponding chapter in Part I.

Introduction

The following is a process recommended for sojourning with a grieving person through their wilderness. Many of the ideas may help and some you may choose not to use. Although they are organized in seventeen steps, please do not be rigid in keeping each step or using them in the exact order. These are meant as guides. Give a copy of the process to the grieving person and discuss it with him or her. If you are a grieving person, give a copy of this process to those who love you and to the one you want to be your sojourner.

Definition of Grief

Grief is a cognitive, emotive, behavioral, and spiritual adjustment period after any loss or lost expectation. It may cause disturbed thought processes, disturbed emotions, disturbed actions/behaviors, and a disturbed spirit for a significant time period. The depth and length of the grief process is in proportion to the meaning and significance of the lost relationship or hope. If the loss is feared to be in the future, grief may be bound up with worry and anxiety.

Definition of a Sojourner

A sojourner is one who has empathy and compassion and is willing to invest time and care with another who is going through grief. A sojourner offers "incarnate care," which means to put into flesh God's love for another. The "sojourner sessions" are designed to help grieving people express and process their emotions, thoughts, behaviors, and spiritual concerns so that they might heal better and not feel so alone. The grieving person must agree to allow the sojourner to walk with them. The following structure offers ideas as to what this time together might be like, but each grieving person and sojourner will need to develop guidelines, which work for both of them.

Guidelines or Steps for the Sojourning Process

1. Ask the grieving person if he or she would like to meet regularly for the purpose of talking about his or her loss, pain, or feared loss. Before you begin, talk about and understand the following guidelines for your sojourning sessions.
2. Meet together regularly. At first, meet as often as the person needs and the sojourner is able. The meeting will need to be more frequent immediately after the loss or tragedy and then usually tapers off as healing takes place. Set limits and talk about limits together. The sojourner also has family and obligations that must be fulfilled.
3. Set up a time for the grief session. Just knowing the meeting is scheduled can help the grieving person feel connected and not so alone.
4. Decide on a place to meet. Find a private place in which you can talk openly and express feelings openly.
5. Encourage the person *not* to mushroom to other subjects. Stay on the subject of his or her grief and loss. Do not let the conversation wonder off just to pass the time or avoid the reality of the pain and grief.
6. Encourage the person to stay in "I" messages, not "you" messages as he or she shares thoughts and feelings. (For example: "I feel sad.")
7. Help the person express his or her honest feelings and thoughts. Don't be shocked by what is said. Just listen while he or she expresses, releases, and catharts the hurt, sadness, anger, frustration, etc.
8. *Do not* try to make the person feel better. *Do not* try to fix him or her or change the subject in order to make the person feel better, or try to make the person laugh or be happy. Just listen.
9. Invite the person to express his or her emotions or have a good cry if needed. Give permission, but do not push. Help the person talk out

his or her feelings rather than you trying to talk him or her out of his or her feelings.

10. If the sojourner does share, keep it short. Be careful that the conversation does not focus on the sojourner's experience. If both of you are grieving, take turns with each having equal time.

11. Never say, "I understand." If you do, then why should the person tell you what you already know? Remember everyone's experience is different even when the situation of loss is the same. Try to say, "Help me understand." The person needs to express it even if you think you already know.

12. Allow for taking a "time-out" or brief breaks during the session as needed, but do not abandon the person. Say, "I need a break. Let's take ten minutes and then start again." If it is at the end of the agreed upon time say, "I need to go now, but let's pick up right here next time."

13. Help the person name is or her needs and what he or she may need from you and others.

14. Help the person explore ways of getting his or her needs met. The sojourner does not provide answers, but helps explore possibilities. All people grieve differently and need different help and support.

15. End the sessions as agreed upon. Don't go on and on. Remember that you, the sojourner, have other responsibilities and a life to live.

16. Set up a time and place for another session before you leave the session. Just knowing this time is scheduled can quiet anxiety and loneliness.

17. Go play. You may play with the person if you are friends. If you are not, go play and live your own life. Don't take the pain home with you. You have limits. If you become absorbed in another's pain, you may soon become exhausted and have little resources to walk with the person through the lengthy wilderness of grief.

Chapter 11

Sojourning with Those in Unbelievable Darkness

Sojourning with the grieving person experiencing darkness, disbelief, shock, or denial is guided by the principles of being present without intrusion and realizing that the individual will move through this in his or her particular way. The questions for the sojourner are: Can I walk with him or her? Can I bear to listen? Can I just sit with the person if need be? Please read Chapter 4, "Unbelievable Darkness," in conjunction with this section. Remember that the shock, denial, and disbelief that bring on the darkness are vehicles and momentary gifts. These gifts momentarily push away reality while the individual is readying the self for facing the unbelievable. The following are some suggestions that may be helpful in ministry to the grieving person.

Be present.

Never underestimate the power of our presence to other people. The Spirit of God and the care that we enflesh through our presence are powerful energies of love and support. Unfortunately, we often doubt and underestimate our value. Remember that our presence is a painful reminder of the reality of their loss. As a result, they may both push us away and, at the same time, want us to stay. At this time they may not know what they want. They just want what has happened not to be real.

They may need to hear the tragic news more than once.

During shock people often do not hear what is said or grasp reality. After being informed of the tragedy, they may not be able to compre-

The Unwanted Gift of Grief: A Ministry Approach
© 2006 by The Haworth Press, Inc. All rights reserved.
doi:10.1300/5644_12

hend nor believe it. They may not hear the doctor use the word cancer or death. The sojourner must move slowly and gently while helping them hear the painful truth. Do not push them too fast, but gently nudge.

Protect them from the environment or from hurting themselves.

They may feel faint or experience other forms of shock. If in any danger, protect them from the surroundings and, if need be, from hurting themselves. They may be in total or partial disequilibrium and need protection until balance returns. For example, if they are running out of the emergency room toward the street, run with them and stop them if they appear to be in danger. If they appear faint, help them to the floor or to a chair. If they need to pace, pace with them. If they hit their heads on walls or floors, try to hold them or use pillows to prevent harm. It is wise to have water and blankets available if they go into chills or feel faint.

Touch, but do not intrude.

Touch can be comforting and helpful. It can also be misunderstood by some or uncomfortable for others. Not everyone is a touch person. If we have known the person prior to the traumatic event, we have a better understanding of what he or she needs. Reading the needs of the person is at the heart of effective sojourning. Move slowly with touch and assess whether he or she experience's it as helpful anchor or as intrusion or restraint. Remember that anything we offer can be misunderstood during this dark experience of the soul.

Gently invite people to talk about the traumatic event and their thoughts and feelings.

In a state of shock, people may not be able to talk or may talk endlessly, rapidly, and anxiously. If possible, help them express what is happening inside them. Help them put into words what they have seen or heard around them. Examples might be: "Can you tell me what your thinking? What are you feeling? When was the last time you saw your wife? Did you and your wife ever talk together about her death? How do you want to tell the children?" Don't allow your anxiety to cause you to ask too many questions, talk too much, or push them too fast. Move slowly, assessing whether talking is what they need at this time. They may need to express the same disbelief many times in an attempt to grasp reality. Try not to get ahead of their ability to grasp but carefully invite them to the next step of reality. This can take time. Sooner or later activities, such as, telling other family members, making funeral decisions, or deciding on treatment plans will invite them to the next step. These decisions may dramatically usher them into dark reality, even though they still experience the event as a bad dream and hope to awake from that dream.

Mirror what they are saying or feeling.

Mirroring people's words and feelings gives them an opportunity to hear what they are saying. In shock, people are not always aware of how or what they are saying. Mirroring may help them hear the reality of their loss and pain. We need to do this with empathy and profound care. Remember people do not want to hear reality, but slowly must face it.

Help them call friends, family, or clergy to be with them or organize a "sit with" group to alternate staying with them during this shocking and dark time.

Individuals in shock may not know who to call or remember routine phone numbers. Our task may be to help them remember or decide. It might be helpful if friends and family take shifts staying with them until the shock and disequilibrium lifts enough so that the person is able to manage self-care.

Follow up with people later on to help them retalk, replay, rethink, or refeel what has happened.

Don't assume that just because the grieving person told us once about the tragic event, she or he does not need to tell us again. It is a common need for individuals to say it over, and over, and over again. This is painful but usually helpful. The verbal rehearsal of the unbelievable event may help the person internalize the unbelievable. Disbelief is usually designed to push away reality. Repeating the tragic story may help the person slowly work it into his or her mind, body, and spirit. Reworking, rethinking, refeeling may help remove the blindfold so eyes can see and ears can hear, yet at the same time, the person does not want to see or hear.

Be aware of those who continue to deny or avoid; they may need professional help.

If people are stuck in long-term denial, they may need help with a professional who understands grief and defense mechanisms. People may slide in and out of acceptance and denial for a long while after loss. The darkness and disbelief can return suddenly. For example, they may continue to hear their loved one's voice in the night or day or wake up not remembering their death. For years, they may refuse to remove clothing, rearrange a room, or go on with life. Over time, the sojourner helps the hurting person talk about these experiences without being forceful or judgmental. This is a delicate ministry. When shock or denial prevents grieving persons from facing reality, they may not be able to go on to use the other vehicles of grief or take the next step toward healing. They may become frozen or stuck in the wilderness.

Prayers, scripture, and religious rituals may be helpful during the darkness and disbelief, but know the person's needs and religious history before you begin these practices.

Prayers offered but not forced may bring comfort and remind people that God cares and is present. On the other hand, these practices may remind them that this event is real. The prayers are about the reality of their loss, tragedy, and need for comfort. Tears may suddenly and uncontrollably flow. Praying with the family around the deceased person's body invites them to participate in a sacred moment and, at the same time, invites the family to begin the journey into the wilderness of grief. Be prepared for people to say "no" to prayers, scriptures, and religious rituals. They may have many reasons for this refusal. In this painful, sacred, and mysterious moment, they may experience religious practices and prayers as intrusive or they may be angry with God and not be able to pray at this time. We need to know the person's needs.

Chapter 12

Sojourning with Those Frustrated and Angry Amid "Why?"

Sojourning with people who are frustrated or angry calls for profound empathy and personal security. Most of us are uncomfortable with frustrated and angry people and tend to avoid them. The sojourner needs to remember that the emotion of anger is not wrong in itself. It is what we do with anger and what anger does with us that may make it complicatedly wrong. Not to express or even to deny frustration or anger can also create problems. These emotions may spoil within and create more depression, implosion, explosion, apathy, isolation, or withdrawal. Please read Chapter 5, "Frustration in the Midst of 'Why?'," in conjunction with this section.

Being with grieving people who are frustrated or angry calls for a deep capacity to listen and offer empathy.

Listening and empathy means that we attempt to see the world through the voice, tears, and eyes of others. This task involves putting aside our agendas and helping people name and express their experiences. These experiences may include frustration and anger. The frustration may be caused by their not feeling that others are listening or trying to understand. When we are willing to sit and listen to their laments, frustration, or anger, they may experience love through us. When we care, they may also experience that God cares. When we listen, they may also experience that God listens. By listening we help people release the pressure and pain under the anger and frustration. When the sojourner listens, the grieving person's frustration and an-

The Unwanted Gift of Grief: A Ministry Approach
© 2006 by The Haworth Press, Inc. All rights reserved.
doi:10.1300/5644_13

ger may become stronger at first before it dissipates and loses its intensity and grip. Help people express it.

Offer verbal and nonverbal grace and permission to be frustrated or angry.

When we let them talk, we are giving them permission. As the sojourner listens, hurting people may begin to apologize for being angry. They may even tell us about their feelings of guilt for expressing frustration, irritability, agitation, or anger. This is a time we can grace them with verbal permission and remind them of the importance of expressing anger in order to make room for other emotions. Thank them for the trust they place in us by sharing openly their thoughts and feelings. We need to provide a trusted and safe relationship where they can say honestly what they feel or think.

Help them understand that their feelings are natural and expected amidst such life-changing crisis.

This does not mean to generalize by telling them that everyone experiences frustration or anger in grief. Not everyone does experience the same emotions or intensity of emotions. Normalizing their experience can help, but be careful not to belittle their particular experience as everyone's experience. This message can add to their experience of frustration. The hope is that they will not conclude that they are going crazy or are forever destined to live in frustration or anger. As sojourners, we need to be careful not to shame, belittle, or explain away their unique experiences. We must hold their frustration or anger in high regard. It may help them to know that others have experienced this sense of frustration and angry anguish. Knowing that faithful people in biblical history such as: Job, the Psalmist, and Jesus, cried out in anguish and frustration may comfort them. These people cried out, "Why?" In the early verses of Psalm 22, one senses the angry anguish of the Psalmist who cried out, "Why have you forsaken me?" Then he asked where God was in the day and the night. When the timing is helpful, the sojourner may want to read these passages of pain with the grief stricken person in order to help them realize that they are not alone in grief's frustration or anger (Psalms 22:1-8 RSV).

Be slow to give an answer when people ask "Why?".

When those in grief ask "Why?" it is important not to suggest that we have the answer. This question is often a vehicle for releasing frustration or perhaps anger that may result from not being able to control life. These emotions and questions may be expressed toward God because God is often perceived as the all-powerful holy one who is in control of life or is suppose to be in control of life. If individual's believe that God is sovereign, omnipotent, and supposed to be in control of life and death, they may momentarily experience profound frustration toward God for "doing" or "allowing" this tragic event. This is especially true when parents watch children suffer or die. We need to help them tell God their honest feelings, thoughts, or questions. We need not have the answer. Often they may feel belittled if we try to give them an answer to the question of "why?". Help them express their emotions as they stand before the mystery of life and death and cannot understand. Explaining the tragedy as being God's will may not be very comforting and may distance them farther from God and us. So many well-meaning people use this explanation in hopes of cheering up and comforting them.

Some clergy have attempted academic answers by discussing with them the various views and theories regarding the will of God. This discussion seems out of place when the person is intensely mourning. Besides, who can explain mystery? I *do not* believe that God causes the death of one's spouse or child for a purpose. I *do* believe that God is with us, crying with us, and carrying us, in order to bring healing and purpose out of loss and pain. God wants to bring purpose out of purposelessness, resurrection out of death, transformation out of lament, mountain out of valley, morning out of mourning, and comfort out of pain. However, these beliefs do not quickly resolve the pain of the sufferer. We need to be slow in challenging people's belief systems if different from ours. Their beliefs may be holding them up momentarily in the crisis. We may conclude their beliefs are "bad" theology or merely a defense mechanism, but to take their beliefs away or challenge their beliefs too quickly may leave them with nothing to hold on to. Usually they cannot receive our well-meaning ideas or beliefs until we have listened closely to them. In the long run it may be helpful for them to realize that God did not "take" their child but God "received" their child. But this realization may take time to accept. In our effort to communicate what we consider to be "good" theology or beliefs, we do not want to interrupt our relationship of support with them. A day may come when they may be able to hear our views.

Be consistently and sometimes stubbornly available to frustrated and angry grieving people.

People who are experiencing frustration, irritability, and/or anger are not easy to be around. Their anger may stir up our anger or cause us to feel uncomfortable. We may become frustrated because they do not make the progress we want to see in their grieving process. As a result, it is tempting to avoid them. It is especially challenging when their anger with God is transferred onto the clergy or lay minister who in their eyes may represent God. This is not an uncommon experience. Clergy and laypersons need to be prepared for this. Their comments to us may be sarcastic and hurtful. We need to anchor our self-esteem and not take this personally. We need to stay faithful by returning again and again. The sojourner's mission in some situations may be to help them express the venom that may be in or under their pain. There is a difference between people who are angry and those who ask us not to return. To continue visiting people, who sincerely do not want a visit, does not honor their free will. By the words "stubbornly available," I do not mean intrusiveness, but I mean not to wear self-esteem on our shirtsleeves. Do not look to angry, grieving people for validation that we are effective sojourners. We need to find validation from within ourselves, from God, and by getting support from others.

When grieving people angrily attack God, the congregation, the health care team, or us, we need not defend them or ourselves.

This is particularly challenging if people attack those we know to have integrity and genuine care. If we minister in a hospital or hospice and are close to the staff, it is easy to slip into defending the staff. Let them express it. Let them say it. We need not agree with their criticisms, but it is important to listen and help them get it off their chests. We need not argue, debate, or defend. Encourage them to raise their questions and angry voice, if need be, to God and tell God directly. God can handle their words and blows. God already knows what is happening in the human heart. God will receive their frustration and anger and return the energy back to grieving people in the form of love and mercy. God deeply understands loss and gave us the gift of grief to be used as a vehicle for healing.

One day we may need to confront angry people as a way of loving them.

After many months or even years, people may be so stuck in anger that they become bitter or continue hurting those who love them. This may mean it is time to confront. To confront means to lay before them what we see. An example of that which may need confrontation might be widowed, single parent's who direct constant impatience, frustration, and anger toward their children. Another example is when anger continues on and on until people are destructive to themselves or others. This may involve driving recklessly, being short-tempered at work, criticizing others, etc. When this happens it may be time to gently but firmly confront them. This confrontation is designed to tell them precisely what their behavior is doing to others and ultimately themselves. Often grieving people are so caught up in fear, anxiety, and pain that they may not be aware of what their behavior is doing to others or themselves. When confronting, be clear and do not generalize, shame, or label. Tell them, "I need to say something, which I think will be painful and make you angrier for awhile." Always do this face-to-face unless impossible. Do not let this confrontation be the last communication before you walk out the door. Use a voice tone of care and words that say, "Let me tell you what I am seeing and let's discuss it." This kind of conversation may also create deeper trust in the relationship with them. Remember that frustration and anger are normal emotions in grief, but can lead to greater problems if not handled well.

If they are experiencing frustration or anger toward themselves in the form of self-blame, remorse, or guilt, help them talk it out and find forgiveness.

Self-blame, remorse, and guilt are not unusual in the grief wilderness. If people blame themselves or expresses guilt and remorse, sojourners often make the mistake of trying to talk them out of these feelings and perceptions. Hurting people need to heal from the inside out. They need to express their remorse, self-blame, and guilt, if indeed this is a part of their experience. At the same time, we do not want to reinforce their self-blame. They need a good word, but only after we have invested the time to understand them. They may need a word of grace and mercy, but we need to remember that grace and mercy take time to internalize. They may need to know that they are not God. At the same time, we cannot rush their grasp of this deep dynamic of mercy. Remember, that our coaching and teaching soaks in slowly and they may not choose to receive it. Words of mercy cannot be internalized until the remorse, regret, self-blame, and guilt are expressed, confessed, and released. This is a process we cannot control and belongs to the Spirit of God and the individual.

Chapter 13

Sojourning with Those
Praying for a Miracle

Being a sojourner with those who are hoping for a miracle is a delicate walk. On one hand, they know the reality of their disease or loss. On the other, they pray for a miracle. They may believe that if they keep faith, the illness will be healed by the next treatment, next doctor, the next prayer, and a miracle. Often, the one who is dying has accepted that death is inevitable, but the family or congregation members have not and may continue to pray for a miracle. Please read Chapter 6, "Praying for a Miracle," in conjunction with this section.

Contracting with God to bring cure or remission through a miracle is normal in the face of loss and especially in the face of dying. There are gifts in reaching and praying for a miracle. One gift is that God can and has given miracles. One's prayers may lead to this gift. Another gift may be the need for a defense or stabilizer against the powerful fear of death or loss of a loved one. This defense against death can lead people to spiritual resources that can enhance medical treatment. For example, hope can lead to prayer, discernment, visualization, worship, meditation, etc. However, in some situations, the hope for a miracle can cause people to deny death and prevent them from using the gift of grief.

If people suppress grief and the reality of death while hoping for a miracle, they may not adequately and faithfully finish life's business on earth and express love and good-byes to the ones they love. For some, hoping for a miracle from God may prevent them from getting needed medical help. For others, if a miracle does not happen, they may feel alone and perhaps rejected, thinking that God has abandoned them.

The Unwanted Gift of Grief: A Ministry Approach
© 2006 by The Haworth Press, Inc. All rights reserved.
doi:10.1300/5644_14

Some may feel guilt that their prayers or faith were not good enough or strong enough in order to obtain the miracle from God.

Accept and understand people's religious and spiritual beliefs, especially if they are different from those of the sojourner.

The first task of sojourning is to develop a relationship of trust with one who grieves. This does not mean that we agree with their beliefs, but means we work to understand the meaning of their beliefs. If we take away or debate their beliefs, they may distance us or feel profoundly misunderstood and vulnerable. Their beliefs have importance to them.

Support and ally both sides of the human and divine dilemma. If people are praying for a miracle, support their hope for physical healing and miracle, but also pray for the miracle of faith and courage to accept whatever the future holds.

We need to be accepting of people's beliefs and even their contracts with God and, at the same time, not ally only with their prayers for miracles. If we pray only for a miracle and it does not take place, then they may not allow us to walk with them into dying and death. The hope of sojourning is to help people embrace both sides of the human and divine dilemma. This dilemma is found in Jesus' experience and prayer in Gethsemane. When we pray, pray both sides of the Gethsemane prayer. We need to pray, "Father, if it be possible, let this cup pass from me ("cure this cancer, grant a miracle") . . . nevertheless, not as I will, but as thou wilt" ("yet, if cure cannot happen give me the courage and faith to face what is ahead") (Mathew 26:39, RSV, my interpretation and additions).

Do not communicate that miracles and healing can only take place if they keep perfect faith—a faith without any doubts.

It is faithful and normal to pray for a miracle and it is faithful and normal to doubt that God will grant a miracle. The important question is, Can we walk with them in both? Can we walk with them without creating the expectation that prayers and faith must be perfect or strong enough in order for God to grant a miracle? Under these requirements, if a miracle does not happen, they may be left with a sense of inadequacy causing them to feel a failure or isolated from God.

When they are ready and able, help them talk about dying and death. Help them recognize that death does not represent failure of faith or God's disfavor of them.

Death does not represent failure. In fact, it may take greater faith to let go and let be and walk through dying and into death than to pray for a miracle and God suddenly grant the miracle. People demonstrate profound faith, when in the fullness of time, they say "yes" to dying and death. We must move at their pace and moments of readiness. If we get ahead of them in this process, they may not allow us to continue to walk the journey with them.

Help them recognize that God is a covenant God. This means that whether they live or die, God is with them.

God's love, mercy, grace, or miracle does not depend on whether our faith is perfect. "It rains on the just and on the unjust" (Mathew 5:45, RSV). Be with them, listen to them, and pray with them if they wish. This may remind them that God has not abandoned them. With our support and care, they may faithfully move to say "yes" to death and courageously walk into death to the eternal presents of God.

Invite them to reflect on scriptures such as Psalm 22, as well as Psalm 23.

Psalm 23 is a favorite passage that reminds us that God is with us in the valley of the shadow of death and loss. This Psalm 22, however, reminds us that even faithful characters of biblical history felt alone and abandoned by God. This Psalm starts with "My God, my God, why hast thou forsaken me? Why are thou so far from helping me, from the words of my groaning? O my God, I cry by day, but thou dost not answer; and by night, but find no rest" (Psalms 22:1-2, RSV). Often people feel abandoned, alone, and inadequate, when the miracle they prayed for does not happen or when they cannot experience the closeness of God. They may need reminders that profound leaders of faith had similar feelings of abandonment and aloneness.

Contracts and bargains with God, spirituality, and/or medical science, can lead the suffering to spiritual and scientific resources, which can indeed facilitate healing and remission of disease.

Contracts and bargains may empower the suffering to search for new methods of treatment and spiritual resources. Their pleads and prayers may lead them to ways of relaxation, meditation, prayer, and/ or religious practices, which actually facilitate healing and help persons manage pain. Studies are available which demonstrate that prayer, spirituality, faith, and religious practices can make medical treatment more effective. However, don't present these spiritual resources as a miraculous panacea. Also, we need to remember that prayers and resources of the mind, body, and spirit can help them say "yes" to death and go through the labor and contractions of dying in a more courageous and less anxious way.

Remember that only when we listen and understand, listen and understand, and listen and understand, do we have the right to speak and be heard.

We may want them to hear and believe our well-meaning suggestions, faith stories, or beliefs, but we need to listen first. Listening enhances trust, rapport, grace, mercy, care, and love in relationships, which prepares their heart and head to hear.

Remember that some persons will continue to plead and contract with God for a miracle and deny that they will die.

They may never come to say "yes" to death. As time moves on, we may witness them becoming more withdrawn. We need to continue visiting them, if they will allow us. Hopefully, our presence will remind them that God is the God of life and of death. Our faithfulness is a symbol that God is a covenant God and will be with them in the valley of the shadow of death and the mountaintop.

***Gently remind them that profound faith is also the capacity
to carry one's pain and know that God walks with them.***

This means we face and faith through dying, amputated body, cancer, or loss. We faithfully face our diseases and carry them. We faithfully walk with a child who has a disability and know that God is with us. We faith and know that God has carved us in the palm of God's hand. When we keep this faith in the midst of death and suffering, it is truly miraculous.

Chapter 14

Sojourning with Those Wrestling with Sadness and Depression

Grief's labor and contractions are never more discouraging than in the desert of sadness and depression. To sojourn with those in this part of the wilderness calls for an understanding of sadness and depression, courage to walk with them, and an abiding level of patience. At this point in the journey, it is not uncommon for the sojourner to feel somewhat helpless in the presence of grieving people. Yet, perhaps now more than any other point of the journey, they need us. Please read Chapter 7, "Wrestling with Sadness and Depression," in conjunction with this section.

Remember, we need not have exact words or answers that lift grieving people out of sadness. Listening and guiding skills are needed to facilitate them into and through the sadness.

Sadness and depression can be an important vehicle for moving through grief. In that sense, they are gifts and the expression of gratitude. Our task is to help them express, release, cathart, and grieve the sadness while they search for new meaning, direction, and future story.

Learn to be comfortable with sadness so that we do not avoid them or their pain.

We often feel uncomfortable with sadness and tears and have a tendency to try and say something that will cheer up grieving people. Do not attempt to talk them out of their feelings, but help them talk out their feelings. Give them permission to cry and, if need be, just be

The Unwanted Gift of Grief: A Ministry Approach
© 2006 by The Haworth Press, Inc. All rights reserved.
doi:10.1300/5644_15

with them in silence while they weep. Human tears are one of the body's most effective antidepressants. Help them cry. Often they have had few friends who are willing or able to do this with them. Reassure them that we will walk with them in the sadness and that their tears will not run us away. If we are not comfortable being with another in their sadness, we may interrupt their healing.

Remember that everyone expresses sadness and depression differently. The reasons are many: personality, family history, culture, gender models and expectations, faith and spiritual beliefs, the perception of their loss, etc.

Try not to let your personal ways of doing and perceiving grief become expectations placed on them. Our ministry is to walk the mile and, at times, the second mile in their shoes of grief. Trust that the Spirit of God and their inner resources will find the way through the wilderness of sadness and depression. Be aware of how their emotions engage our own emotions and sense of helplessness. When their pain engages our sadness, it may cause us to impatiently push them. Do not assume that what helped us will help them. For that matter don't assume that their perceptions and emotional responses to loss will be the same as ours.

Be aware of their pathways for expressing grief and relate first to their view of the world. Be aware as to whether they tend to think through grief, feel through grief, or take action through grief.

See the chapter on differences in the grief wilderness where this is clarified more in depth. If he or she tends to be a *thinking person,* begin by inviting the person to use more cognitive ways of communicating grief such as, "What thoughts came into your mind when you went into your daughter's empty bedroom?" Or if we are with a *feel person,* start by asking about his or her feelings. "What feelings did you have when you went into your daughter's empty bedroom?" Or if we are with an *act person* who tends to take action with his or her pain, we may want to ask about behaviors and actions. "What did you do when you went into your daughter's empty bedroom?" Optimal healing takes place when we use all of the pathways given to us by God. People are created with the ability to think, feel, and act. As rapport and trust develop, we may then want to slowly invite them to use and express the pathways of grieving that they tend to avoid. Emptying out into another's perspective means starting with their preferred pathway for grieving.

Help grieving people identify and express their feelings and thoughts below the surface. Invite them to go deeper if they can.

People often express the emotions most readily and consciously available to them. While expressing these emotions, they may not express or even be aware of the emotions that are under the surface. For example, men often express anger and frustration when they may be experiencing sadness and depression underneath the anger. Sadness and depression may not be as socially acceptable expressions for a man. For example, women often express sadness and depression when they may be experiencing frustration or anger underneath the sadness and depression. Frustration or anger may not be as socially acceptable expressions for a woman. These are tendencies and, therefore, not true of every woman or man. Each may need to look under the obvious in order to talk about their underlying thoughts or emotion. The sojourner needs to move gracefully and not get in a hurry with rapid questions. Our gentle objective is to invite them to express all of these emotions if they are able and if they desire. These are invitations not intrusions. These invitations are usually more effective when the sojourner has listened long and empathically and trust is established in the relationship.

The following are examples of possible invitations. If they cannot go deeper then do not push.

- "Please help me understand. Tell me more about that."
- "What was it like last night when you realized that?"
- "Could you tell me about your daughter? What was she like? When do you miss her the most?"
- "Are there any other thoughts or feelings with your sadness?"
- "Are there any other thoughts or feelings with your anger/ frustration?"

***When their depression level is deeper or more complicated
than we are able to understand or attend, encourage them
to seek professional help. Offer to go with them if need be.***

See the chapter on sadness and depression and review the symptoms of clinical depression. Know these symptoms and listen for them, especially if people are expressing suicidal thoughts. This means thoughts of not wanting to live or wanting to hurt themselves. Take these comments seriously. Encourage them to get profession help immediately. In normal grief, the emotional journey may cause chemistry changes in the body, mind, and spirit that may need medical evaluation and treatment. The stress of profound grief can create and contribute to disease and dis-ease. If we do make a referral to a professional, be sure not to abandon them. Continue to ask how they are doing and listen. Don't abandon them because of our own feelings of helplessness or incompetence. Often, they already feel abandoned by God, their deceased loved one, and others.

***Grief's sadness and depression can go on and on. People
may need to reexpress, replay, reexperience, and research
the meaning of the tragic event over and over until they
transform toward healing. Help them do this.***

Be prepared to listen because talking is how many do their grief work toward healing. This is especially true for extroverts. We may be exhausted from hearing the same stories, but, I assure you, they are more exhausted and sick of saying it and feeling it. The human mind, emotions, body, and spirit are amazing and complex mechanisms. To let go of the past and, at the same time, internalize the past and move into the future is complex and hard work. This often involves rehearsing and repeating the story of loss and pain. Help them talk it out. This is an awesome gift to give.

Chapter 15

Sojourning with Those
in Healing and Light

When grief finally gives birth to new life, the task of the sojourner is to celebrate with them, assure them, and at times caution grieving people. As they move into significant acceptance, healing, and light, they will be trying out their wings with new activities, interest, and relationships. These new experiences can bring moments of euphoria, sadness, and fear. This is a time when people often do not make the best decisions. Please read Chapter 8, "Healing: Experiencing the Light Again," in conjunction with this section.

When grieving people are ready to focus on new activities, interests, and relationships, help them process the meaning, thoughts, feelings, joys, and fears related to these new changes.

When we learn to walk again there is a tendency to both fear taking a fall and, at the same time, a tendency to hurry, wanting to do everything at once. In the early stages of acceptance and healing, euphoria may push them to make premature decisions that may not be good decisions in the long run. For example, upon dating again the widower may suddenly fall in love and want to get married. However, the relationship may be only a transitional relationship. As sojourners we have no right to control their decisions, but can hopefully help them process decisions closely before action is taken. Explore the following questions. What does this new event or relationship mean? What will it do for them in the long run? Is this a decision that they can delay

The Unwanted Gift of Grief: A Ministry Approach
© 2006 by The Haworth Press, Inc. All rights reserved.
doi:10.1300/5644_16

until further healing takes place? Help them come to their own decisions regarding the future, but we may need to help them examine and slow down finalizing decisions. Remind them that in the midst of healing, the grieving may attempt to make major decisions too quickly and later regret them.

As people stretch their wings, they will not need the sojourners as often or in the same way.

At some point in the process, the sojourner may actually remind them of their painful past and their dependency needs during the painful wilderness. Now they are ready to go on. This process is healthy weaning. This is normal in human development and in healing development during grief. The goal of life is to grow into interdependence, not just independence. During this transformation process people may experience ambivalence toward the sojourner. They may know they need us and, at the same time, don't want to need us. This is a time we need to be accepting, sensitive, and encouraging, while offering important space for them to create their future.

It may be time to redefine your relationship.

If your relationship prior to the grief wilderness was that of business associate, friend, or tennis partner, talk about how you both can now focus more on playing tennis or doing friend things. Sojourners will not need to meet with them as often, or at all, for grief work purposes. Let them call if they need us. At the same time, we need not abandon them. Keep asking how they are doing or how the date went the night before. If in the wilderness of grief they viewed the sojourner as a buoy in stormy waters, now the task is to become fellow swimmers again. Be sure your own need to be needed does not keep them from differentiating from you, so that they can go on with their lives. They will make mistakes. Hopefully, they will let you explore with them the mistakes, failures, and successes of this new freedom. They will find their way not our way. The role and goal of the sojourner is to mid-wife the grieving person into new life and then let go and let be.

As grieving people move from early acceptance toward significant healing, they will experience less euphoria, impulsiveness, neediness, and roller coastering. Life will become an invitation again and they will feel less driven. If they will let you, walk with them through to this light.

When they get to this point of harmony, constancy, and depth of healing, we have witnessed the results of the gift of grief. Now our role as sojourner recycles toward colleague and friend. We have witnessed how the mystery of God's Spirit, the human spirit, and love heals. They transform into new life and their future story. They walk autonomously into the light and more effectively see through things. This is a time for gratitude and celebration. This is the evidence of things previously unseen in the wilderness of grief. And yet, even as they go on with life, they do not want to forget and, at times, will reexperience grief and loss. Perhaps this will be during special events, seasons, anniversaries, or birthdays. We need to remember them and ask how they are doing.

PART IV:
MORE WAYS TOWARD
TRANSFORMATION

Chapter 16

Marriage:
Tough Enough Without Grief

Marriage is filled with joys, challenges, growth opportunities, and times of struggle. In marriage seminars I humorously say, "There are three ways to get therapy—employ a therapist, get married, and have children." They are all expensive and all hard work. All three will call you to grow and learn about yourself in ways that you never imagined possible. Our spouse is our teacher, but we must be willing to learn. We are our spouse's teacher, but he or she must be willing to learn. We learn and grow together.

COUPLES AND GRIEVING

Marriage is tough enough without grief. When a dramatic loss or trauma comes to families and intimate relationships, it can shake the ground of being together. Losses take many forms. The loss of a child or the birth of a child with a handicap can throw both spouses into grief. The relationship is suddenly faced with emotional overload. The loss of a job can be a profound self-esteem loss for the one who is laid off and can bring fear and anxiety for both spouses facing the possibility of losing financial security. The loss of a spouse or a parent to death or a serious illness can cause dramatic changes in the family and marriage relationship.

Of the losses I have observed, the loss of a child seems to have the most profound effect on a marriage and family. I received a telephone

The Unwanted Gift of Grief: A Ministry Approach
© 2006 by The Haworth Press, Inc. All rights reserved.
doi:10.1300/5644_17

call from Caroline, a young wife and mother. She received my name from a friend. This conversation took place more than twenty-five years ago, but I remember it as if it were yesterday.

After introducing herself, Caroline told me that her two-year-old son was killed and that she needed to talk about his death and the effects on the relationship with her husband, Daniel. She took a deep breath and through tears, told me the painful story.

Her son, Davy, was killed three months before. Daniel was backing out of the driveway one morning to go to work and somehow, with neither of them knowing, the child ran behind the car. The young father ran over little Davy and killed him.

Caroline went on, "Chaplain, it was not Daniel's fault. He had no idea that Davy was outside. I should have known. I should have been watching. If anything, it was my fault." She cried gasping for breath. I listened and encouraged her to continue. As expected, Daniel had been depressed since the tragedy. He felt totally responsible. He blamed himself. Caroline said that at first she was able to reassure her husband that it was not his fault.

After the accident, Daniel withdrew from her and then slowly she withdrew from him. She said, "Chaplain, he goes off by himself and just stares. I try to talk with him and he won't respond. If I cry around him he feels worse. He says nothing and goes off to the next room. In bed he reaches out for me and I can't respond to his sexual needs. Now he often misses work and drinks too much. Now neither of us has the motivation to do anything."

This was a tragic situation. After we talked for an hour or so, I made a referral to a marriage therapist who was near them and one who understood grief and its effects on marriage. This couple had a lot of grief work, marriage work, and wilderness ahead of them and needed a compassionate and skilled guide.

Not every loss in marriage and family is this dramatic or traumatic. We often try to convince ourselves that loss and grief would never affect our marriages. Hopefully that is true, but we all would be surprised at the effects of loss, trauma, and grief on intimate relationships. Loss of health, the diagnosis of cancer, the birth of child with a handicap, death of a child or stillborn infant, loss of a job, death of a parent, etc., all have unexpected effects on our relationships.

What makes grief so difficult to manage in our intimate relationships? Following are some reasons, although my comments will not be true about every marriage. They are not true for every woman or every man, since everyone grieves differently. You will want to read Chapter 2, "Everyone Grieves Differently," and Chapter 3, "Factors that Affect the Wilderness of Grief," to better understand why people grieve differently.

Grief Factors That Affect Marriage

Many factors of how grief affects marriage may not be discussed here, but I have found the following to be important. When I use the word *tendency* or *tends,* I mean that we may observe general behaviors that are true for one gender or the other. There are many exceptions. The exceptions are based on a person's history and role models that taught him or her to relate, love, and grieve. Much of what you are about to read is based on my own observations of couples working through grief. Many of my comments are influenced by writings of those who have studied closely the behaviors of men and women. When applied to grieving, I am not suggesting that their conclusions would agree with my conclusions. However, they have contributed significantly to my understanding of marriage and gender differences.[1]

GENDER DIFFERENCES AND GRIEVING

The following are brief clarifications of male and female differences and tendencies as each go through the wilderness of grief. These are dynamics and behaviors that I have observed in marriage counseling. Remember, these are tendencies and not always true about every man or every woman. I am sure you could add tendencies not included.

- Where women tend to do grief in connection and relationship with others, men tend to do grief within themselves and often by themselves.
- Where women tend to be more emotionally expressive of grief, men tend to be more cognitively expressive and share fewer emotions of grief.

- Where women tend to do more nurturing as a way of helping during grief, men tend to do more guiding and providing as a way of helping during grief.
- Where women tend to talk about their loss and grief openly, men tend to withdraw verbally or talk about other things.
- Where culture tends to expect and permit women to be tender, emotive, and sensitive while grieving, culture tends to expect and permit men to be tough, in control, and put up a brave front while grieving. (Fortunately these social expectations on gender are changing.)
- Where women tend to want to be cherished by men during grief, men tend to want to be needed by women during grief. As a result, they both may want to help the other feel better, but may innocently miss each other's needs.
- Where women tend to use the pathways of sadness, hurt, and depression through grief, men tend to use the pathways of frustration, anger, and irritable impatience.
- When women express sadness, hurt, and depression in grief, men tend to respond with frustration, anger, and irritable impatience to the woman's sadness, hurt, and depression. When men express frustration, anger, and irritable impatience in grief, women tend to respond with sadness, hurt, and depression to the man's frustration, anger, and irritable impatience. This can become a cycle that feeds misunderstanding and more distance between them. The more he expresses anger and frustration, the more she feels hurt, sad, unhelpful, and misunderstood. The more she expresses sadness and hurt, the more he feels frustrated, angry, unhelpful, and misunderstood. I call this the distance-escalating cycle.
- Where women tend to be helped more by being with others and talking about their grief and emotions, men tend to be helped more by being with others and participating in activities with them (fishing, golf, sports, etc.), and usually do not talk about their grief or emotions openly.
- Where women tend to listen, understand, and make suggestions to help the man through grief, men tend to listen, identify the problem, and try to fix or solve the problem to help women through grief. Both are thinking they are being helpful.

- Where women tend not to feel understood or comforted when the man tries to fix or solve their loss or grief, men tend to experience suggestions from the woman as belittling their ability to deal with loss or grief.
- Where women tend to fear abandonment because of a man's lack of emotional availability and response to their grieving, men tend to fear being smothered by women's emotional and supportive response to their grieving.
- Where women tend to become emotional and physical caregivers to a sick child or parent, men tend to give advice or provide for giving care to the sick child or parent.
- Where women tend to emotionalize their sexual needs during grief, men tend to sexualize their emotional needs during grief.

It is no wonder we find distance and misunderstanding creeping into our marriages that add to the normal adjustments faced in loss and grief. These dynamics and behaviors can escalate distance. Once in the cycle our relationships need to give special attention to break the cycle. If you look closely, you probably find that the roles previously discussed are also seen in other family relationships, such as: father and daughter, mother and son, brother and sister.

Reconciling Our Different Needs

I am often asked in marriage counseling and grief seminars, "Which is the best way to grieve?" You probably can guess my response. I recommend that couples appreciate their differences and meet in the middle. Meet in the middle of your different ways of needs and ways of grieving. Find the middle and take turns alternating between her ways of needing to grieve and his ways of needing to grieve. For example, if one wants to go to the cemetery on Saturday and the other wants to go to a movie, work to make both happen. If one wants to sit, talk, and cry and the other wants to withdraw in front of the computer or at the golf range, work to make both happen. If one wants to have sex and the other wants to only be held, work to make both happen. Find the middle. The middle is the middle of what both think is the middle. This is what makes finding the middle such hard work. This effort toward mutuality is what makes marriage fulfilling and couple grieving more intimate.

Mutuality in Grieving

Because your spouse grieves differently than you, does not mean he or she is doing grief ineffectively. Nor do these differences mean that your spouse does not love you. Misunderstandings and problems can arise when both insist that the other grieve his or her way. This can create hurt, distance, and misunderstanding that can become embedded in the relationship. When couples refuse to meet in the middle or take turns to help each get their needs met, than distance and isolation may lead to dying love or embedded impasse. As time moves on, you may not only be grieving over the loss that precipitated your painful journey, but also grieving the loss of love in the marriage. Marriage and grieving are hard work.

Marriage is tough enough without grief. I invite you both to the hard work of marriage and grief. You both can make it through these tough times to comfort and healing. You both can come out, on the other side of the wilderness of grief, with a stronger marriage and deeper understanding of life. As a result, you will become more empathic and compassionate. Perhaps you will become wounded healers for other couples going through loss and grief.

Marriage is recognized as a sacrament in many faith traditions. There are varied definitions for the word sacrament. I define sacrament as a physical sign of the real presence of God. In marriage, we are a physical sign of the real presence of God to each other. This God loves us and mourns with us when we mourn. We are called to mourn with each other along the journey of life, as well as, celebrate with each other along the journey of life.

COMPLEMENTARITY IN MARRIAGE AND GRIEF

One of the reasons we marry is to have complementarity in our lives. This intimate help mate and soul mate embodies love to us and brings us wholeness and more completion. In my observations, we tend to choose others who are different than we are in order to find this completion and love. Much of what one spouse may not be able to do well, another may be able to accomplish very well. This also tends to be true about our personalities, weaknesses and strengths, and introvertness and extrovertness. This mutual mission has a mysterious and joyful synergy of its own, when a couple can bless it and affirm it. The real challenge is to stay in complementarity and stay out of competition with one another.

In grief, this complementarity is a mysterious spiritual resource, but at times can be painful. We grieve differently than our spouse, but also our spouse can model and encourage us to use more than one pathway through grieving. As a result we may be able to grieve more completely, fully, and helpfully. Our spouse is our teacher and that in itself is challenging to accept. Marriage includes love and conflict and both can hone and shape us toward growth. If you want to know how you need to change and grow, just ask your spouse.

Spouses can teach each other how to more effectively get through the wilderness of grief. A man may need a woman to teach him and permit him to be more expressive of tenderness, sadness, hurt, and emote openly in grief. A woman may need a man to teach her and permit her to be more expressive of toughness, frustration, and anger in grief. Both are important pathways to healing. We need each other. The hope of marriage is that we learn from each other and grow because of each other. It is in bringing our differences to the relationship and celebrating our differences, that we become one body and one communion of love. This communion can see us through dark nights of the soul.

THE GIFT OF SEXUAL CLOSENESS AMID GRIEF

At the heart of the profound sacrament of marriage is the gift of sexual love, closeness, expression, and renewal. In grief our sexual needs are different. For that matter, sexual needs and expression are different for each lover in every marriage. Marriage is a lifetime of finding the middle of both persons' needs. The rhythms of sexuality change in a lifetime together and also change dramatically during times of profound grief.

During the grief, wilderness sexual experiences can be a spiritual resource and a repulsion, an emotional nurturance and a depletion, or a communion and a conflict. Each lover has different needs and expression. Sexual closeness is physical, spiritual, and emotional. Sexual mutuality is a powerful gift that created the child that today may have died. Sexual mutuality is also a powerful gift that helps recreate the spirit of two broken hearts after loss. Sacred sexuality, with its touch and embrace, can be a physical release from grief buried in the human heart, a balm of comfort amidst pain, a calming amidst the storm, a respite from mourning into a communion of closeness, and an unexplainable nurturing and feeding of the human soul. Sexuality can be a gift amid the helpful wilderness of grief.

APPENDIX: THE GRIEF DATE— A GUIDE FOR COUPLES AND FAMILY MEMBERS

In my counseling practice with couples and other family members, I often invite them to go on grief dates together. On this particular date the purpose is to talk about loss and grieve together and not avoid the pain or subject. First, I teach couples how to be on a grief date and set up one or two of these dates. When they return the next week, we talk about the date(s) and I explore with them their feelings and thoughts related to the experience. I also coach as to how they could make it more effective. These grief dates bring them closer together and provide a way to stay attuned and connected with one another.

I also strongly encourage them to have other kind of dates during the week. Fun dates, conflict-resolution dates, romantic dates, etc. I try to help them understand that the grief date is only for grieving and talking about their loss. The following is a guide for helping couples with the "grief date." You will find instructions and a step-by-step process for making this grief date meaningful and helpful. Remember the goal is not to talk each other out of grief, but help each other talk out grief while supporting one another. In the early weeks and months after a loss, you may want to meet every day for awhile. In the first few days you may want to meet as often as you need to talk and cry. But as the months pasts you will probably notice that you don't need a grief date as often. Don't be surprised if after you try this a few times, you both begin to look forward to your grief date together, feel closer, and more understood. From my clients I have learned that this makes other types of dates more fun and meaningful as well. Give your marriage and your grief your best effort and hard work.

Helping Relationships Mourn and Make It Through the Wilderness of Grief

Introduction

The following is a process recommended for couples in which one or both have experienced a significant loss and are in a wilderness of grief. Although the guidelines are organized in steps, please do not be rigid about using each step or in the exact order. These are meant as guides. I suggest you discuss this process together before you use it and have a copy available when you meet.

Definition of Grief

Grief is a cognitive, emotive, behavioral, and spiritual adjustment period after any loss or disappointed expectation. It may cause disturbed thought processes, disturbed feelings, disturbed actions/behaviors, and a disturbed spirit for a significant time period. The depth and length of the grief process is usually in proportion to the meaning and significance of the lost person or hope. If the loss is in the future but threatening, grief may be bound up with added worry and anxiety. Because everyone experiences grief differently, couples, family members, or close friends may find that they do not understand each other. This process is designed to help these unique relationships.

Definition of a Grief Date

Just as we set up dates for fun, romance, and to accomplish shared tasks, the grief date is designed to help close family and friend relationships come together to talk and do grief work. This process can involve more than two people who are friends or family members. The grief date is a time of listening and talking alternately. This date, as with all dates, calls for empathy, compassion, and patience. The grief date is designed to help the participants express and process their feelings, thoughts, behaviors, and spiritual concerns so that they might heal better and not feel so alone. If your loved one will not meet with you, please try to use these suggestions as best you can.

Guidelines or Steps for the Grief Date

1. Talk together about these guidelines and agree to them in principle before you start the process.
2. Grieve together regularly. At first meet as often as possible. The dates are more frequent immediately after a loss or tragedy and then taper off over the months as healing takes place.
3. Set up a time for the grief date. Ask for time to grieve together. Just knowing the meeting is scheduled can help you feel connected and not so alone.
4. Decide on a place to meet. Find a private place in which you can talk openly and express feelings openly.

5. Do not mushroom to other subjects. Encourage each other to stay on the subject of grief and loss. Do not let the conversation wander off to other subjects.

6. Stay in "I" messages not "you" messages when you share thoughts or feelings. ("I feel sad" rather than "You feel sad when this happens.")

7. Express your honest feelings and thoughts to one another. Take turns talking. Listen while the other expresses the hurt, sadness, anger, frustration, etc.

8. *Do not* try to make your partner feel better. *Do not* try to fix him or her or change the subject in order to make the person feel better, laugh, or be happy. Just listen.

9. Invite and help your partner talk out his or her feelings rather than try to talk him or her out of feelings. Give your partner permission to feel what he or she feels or thinks.

10. Keep a balance between talking and listening. Take turns with fairly equal time for each.

11. Never say, "I understand." If you do, then why should your partner tell you what you already know? Remember, everyone's experience of grief is different even when the type of loss is the same. Try to say, "Help me understand." They need to express it even if you think you already know.

12. Allow for taking a needed "time-out" or brief breaks during the session but do not abandon or cut off sharing. Say, "I need a break. Let's take ten minutes and then start again." If it is at the end of the agreed upon time say, "Let's talk some more about this tomorrow." Set up a time for this.

13. Name your needs and what you need from each other.

14. Meet in the middle. You both have different needs. You both grieve differently. Work to meet each other's needs in the middle.

15. End your date and leave the grief the best you can, until your next date. Go play, work, and love together. Enjoy and be grateful for each other.

16. Enjoy and be grateful for each other. Express appreciation for the individual and the time together, in spite of the pain the session brings.

17. Set up another date at the end of this session or ask for a date the next time the loss on grief is felt.

Chapter 17

Ways of Making it Through
the Wilderness of Grief

So many ask, "How can I make it through this?" The following ideas may not help every grieving person make it through the wilderness of grief. We all grieve differently and we are helped in different ways. Some ideas and activities may be more helpful than others, based on your unique grief, needs, and situation. These suggestions come from those who have been through grief. I have recommended many of these in grief counseling. Please remember, these are not offered as ways to take your pain away, but ways to help you go into and through your pain to healing and hope.

1. Find a sojourner to walk with you. Give him or her the sojourner chapters and guide in this book. If the sojourner is not familiar with grief, give him or her a copy of this book. Your sojourner may or may not be a professional, but needs to be a sensitive listener.
2. Eat, sleep, and exercise well, even though you may have little interest in them right now.
3. Do not be embarrassed to cry. Crying can be a great healer and a natural antidepressant to the mind, body, and spirit. It takes courage and strength to cry, especially to cry openly with others.
4. Plan and structure your time, but try not to overstructure your time. Leave time for grieving and practicing being alone.
5. Remember that your grief is gratitude. Do not let anyone take it away.

The Unwanted Gift of Grief: A Ministry Approach
© 2006 by The Haworth Press, Inc. All rights reserved.
doi:10.1300/5644_18

6. Get involved in an effective support group. Attend four times before you make your decision as to whether to return. Some report that they do not at first feel comfortable at these meetings.

7. Do not be concerned if for a long while your prayers, activities, or thoughts lead you to thinking and feeling about your pain and loss.

8. Try not to make any major decisions about your life for at least the next eighteen months, unless it is a necessity. If a necessity, first get consultation from trusted friends or professionals.

9. Get your hands busy doing something and your mind and spirit will began to follow them. Even though you have little interest in your hobby now, give it a little time each day. Perhaps you could try cleaning the house a little at a time.

10. If your partner is grieving or both of you are grieving at the same time, invite him or her on a grief date and use the guidelines found in the chapter on marriage.

11. Get your mind busy learning something. Focus on a book, a new class or seminar, a newspaper, etc. You may not be able to focus for long periods of time, but start a little at a time.

12. Read about grief or attend a grief seminar, so you will understand that although you feel you are going crazy, you are not going crazy. You are in the wilderness of grief.

13. Learn and practice slow breathing, centering prayer, prayer, meditation, or visualize a hopeful future story. Your mind and spirit will often follow.

14. Journal or write down anything you think or feel. Give yourself permission to misspell, write messy, and make grammar mistakes. When you sit to write, let the words and thoughts go where they go. Let go and follow your mind, spirit, and pen. This time of writing may become a comforting friend and a healing experience.

15. Use clay, paints, pencil drawings, etc., to express your thoughts and feelings. Be messy. Don't critique your creation.

16. Permit yourself *not* to go through your grief perfectly. Be aware that too high a self-expectation can block and frustrate you.

17. Grieve openly with those you trust and those who care. Beware of those who try to cheer you up all the time. If they are trying to avoid your pain or their own, you may not want to open up to them regularly.

18. If need be, cry every day for forty-five minutes or even fifteen minutes, and then stand up and tackle life.

19. When you are frustrated and angry, yell, scream, holler, or hit a pillow for ten minutes. You may want to do this alone if those around you cannot handle it. Children may be frightened of this activity seen in a parent. However, you may want to teach them to do this if need be.

20. Tell your friends what you need. Ask them to just listen for a while. Tell them that they need not have answers nor cheer you up. Give them a copy of the sojourner process, which gives them ideas of what helping looks like.

21. Develop your spirituality. Spirituality is the capacity to see through things toward transcendence and deeper meaning. It may lead you to a Holy Comforter and Sustainer.

22. Develop your humor. Humor is the capacity to see through things toward transcendence and deeper meaning.

23. Develop your wisdom. Wisdom is the capacity to see through things toward transcendence and deeper meaning.

24. Use spirituality, humor, and wisdom to get through these tough days.

25. Encourage yourself to be in a crowd, even if at the same time you are feeling alone or lonely.

26. In the months ahead, life will invite you to make changes. Come to believe that change is an opportunity for growth and creating a future story.

27. Call or visit with others who have been through grief and perhaps your particular kind of loss. Ask them about their experiences and how they made it through.

28. When you date again or if you date again, take it slow. Enjoy dating and sharing, but remember that your deep needs for intimacy and connection may lead you to make quick decisions. These quick decisions may not be the best decisions in the long run.

29. Walk or do some other exercise not just for fitness, but also as a way to release the emotional pain that can saturate your body, mind, and spirit.

30. Reframe your negative thoughts into positive affirmations and repeat them to yourself over and over every day. For example, if you keep thinking, "I will never make it through this," real-

istically rewrite the negative thought to say, "It will be difficult, but I will make it through this."

31. Come to believe that God did not cause this tragedy for a purpose, but will be with you to find a meaningful purpose out of
this tragedy.

32. Remember that God did not take your child or loved one, but
received him or her.

33. When holidays or anniversaries come, structure activities and
schedule time with people you love, but do not overstructure
the time. The first year or so you may want to schedule time to
grieve, cry, and reflect during these special occasions.

34. Think back over your life when you were in tough times before and remember that somehow you made it through. What
helped in the past?

35. Remember everyone uses different pathways through grief.
Some people *think through* grief to new feelings and actions,
some people *feel through* grief to new thoughts and actions,
and some people stay busy *through* grief to new feelings and
thoughts. Everyone grieves differently. I suggest you use all
three of these God-given pathways.

36. Go on and love others more fully because you have been loved
by your deceased loved one.

37. Pray openly and honestly to God. God already knows your
heart, so you need not put up a good front. Tell God what you
think and feel.

38. Grief is a great memorial and tribute to your deceased loved
one. But the ultimate memorial and tribute to him or her is
when you go on to love life and others more fully because he
or she loved you.

39. If you feel blocked and cannot seem to move through grief,
employ a competent and sensitive counselor or coach that understands grief.

40. If you and your physician agree that you need medication(s)
in order to help you through this, do not let your friends talk
you out of it or put you on a guilt trip. At the same time, don't
allow your physician to overmedicate you. You want to feel
enough pain so you can do your grief work, yet also continue
to function at home and at work.

41. Talk openly about all your emotions—shock, frustration, anger, sadness, depression, helplessness, hopelessness, etc., with someone you trust.

42. Schedule breakfast, lunch, dinner, or coffee with a friend at your favorite restaurant. It is appropriate that for awhile this may bring pain or uneasiness.

43. Practice going out to eat alone from time to time. Some day it may feel like solitude rather than loneliness.

44. Grief may erupt more powerfully or suddenly when you attend worship or other congregation activities. This is normal. Take it slow in reentering life's activities, but also courageously keep nudging yourself to do more as the months pass.

45. When you read scripture, read not only the promises of making it through trying times (such as Psalm 23), but also read about biblical characters who felt the pain you feel. For example, read the opening verses of Psalm 22, the story of Job or Jesus in Gethsemane. You are not alone!

46. Watch a favorite movie or listen to a favorite music selection and just have a good cry. Some day the tears will not be as abundant. Do not let your tears be buried within because this may slow down the healing process.

47. Do not let good-intentioned friends rush you into resurrection and feeling good. Strength can develop when we stay in grief and Gethsemane awhile.

48. Remember that when you do not know how to pray, your grieving, mourning, and groaning is your prayer to God. The Spirit translates your groaning to God who knows your pain and needs.

49. Remember that faith does not mean having to smile away your pain, but means facing and walking into your pain. Faith means to use God's gift of grief in order to heal.

50. Remember that God mourns with you.

Make a list of other ideas that others have shared or ideas and activities you find helpful in getting through grief. Repeat them often! These are not offered as ways to take your pain away, but ways to help you go into and through your pain to healing, hope, and transformation to new life.

Notes

Chapter 2

1. David Augsburger, *Pastoral Counseling Across Cultures* (Philadelphia: Westminster Press, 1986).

Chapter 3

1. C. W Brister, Pastoral Ministry Professor and my mentor at Southwestern Baptist Theological Seminary, first introduced me to this graceful concept. This had a profound effect on my perception of a God of covenant.

2. Erik Erikson, *Identity and the Life Cycle* (New York: W. W. Norton & Com., 1980).

Chapter 6

1. Herbert Benson, *The Relaxation Response* (New York: Avon Books, 1976); Joan Borysenko, *Minding the Body, Mending the Mind* (New York: Bantam Books, 1988); Larry Dossey, *Healing Words: The Power of Prayer and the Practice of Medicine* (New York: HarperCollins, 1993); Harold Koenig, Michael McCullough, and David Larson, *Handbook of Religion and Health.* (New York: Oxford University Press, 2001); and Elisabeth McSherry, "The Scientific Basis of Whole Person Medicine," *Journal of American Scientific Affiliation* 35, (4) (1983), pp. 217-224. For more resources see suggested reading.

2. Claudia Kalb, "God & health: Is religion good medicine? Why science is starting to believe in faith & healing," *Newsweek,* CXLII (19) (November 10, 2003), pp. 44-56.

3. Morton Kelsey, *Healing and Christianity* (Minneapolis MN: Augsburg Fortress Press, 1995).

4. Elisabeth Kübler-Ross, *On Death and Dying* (New York: Macmillan, 1969).

Chapter 10

1. Carl Rogers, *A Way of Being* (Boston: Houghton Mifflin, 1980), p. 137.
2. Ibid., p. 142.

The Unwanted Gift of Grief: A Ministry Approach
© 2006 by The Haworth Press, Inc. All rights reserved.
doi:10.1300/5644_19

Chapter 16

1. The research and writing of the following authors have added to my under-standing of women and men. They have stretched my thoughts, counseling theories, and practice as I work with couples and individuals. Carol Gilligan, *In a Different Voice* (Cambridge, MA: Harvard University Press, 1981); John Gray, *Men Are from Mars: Women Are from Venus* (New York: HarperCollins, 1992); Harville Hendrix, *Getting the Love You Want* (New York: H. Holt & Company, 2001); and Deborah Tannen, *You Just Don't Understand* (New York: Morrow, 1990).

Suggested Reading

Augsburger, David. *Caring Enough to Confront: How to Understand and Express Your Deepest Feelings Toward Others.* Ventura, CA: Regal Press, 1973.

Benson, Herbert. *Beyond the Relaxation Response.* New York: Berkley, 1985.

_____. *Timeless Healing: The Power and Biology of Belief.* New York: Scribner, 1996.

_____. *Your Maximum Mind.* New York: Times Books, 1987.

Borysenko, Joan. and Miroslav Borysenko. *The Power of the Mind to Heal: Reviewing Body, Mind, and Spirit.* Carlsbad, CA: Hay House Inc., 1994.

Brister, C.W. *Change Happens: Finding Your Way Through Life's Transitions.* Macon, GA: Peake Road, 1997.

_____. *Pastoral Care in the Church,* Third Edition, Revised. San Francisco: Harper, 1992.

_____. *Take Care.* Nashville: Broadman, 1978.

Buscaglia, Leo. *The Fall of Freddie the Leaf.* New York: Charles B. Slack, Inc., 1982.

Caine, L. *On Being a Widow.* New York: William Morrow & Co, 1974.

Capps, Donald. *Life Cycle Theory and Pastoral Care.* Philadelphia: Fortress Press, 1983.

Claypool, John. *Tracks of a Fellow Struggler.* New Orleans, LA: Insight Press, First Edition, 1974, Revised Edition, 1995.

_____. *The Saga of Life: Living Gracefully Through All the Stages,* Revised Edition. Harrisburg, PA: Morehouse Publishers, 2002.

Clinebell, Howard. *Basic Types of Pastoral Counseling: Resources for Ministry of Healing and Growth,* Revised and Enlarged. Nashville: Abingdon Press, 1984.

Cousins, Norman. *Anatomy of an Illness.* New York: W.W. Norton, 1979.

_____. *The Healing Heart.* New York: Avon Books, 1984.

Dossey, Larry. *Space, Time and Medicine.* Boston: Shambhala Publications, 1982.

Egan, Gerard. *The Skilled Helper.* Pacific Grove, CA: Brooks/Cole Publ. Co., 2002.

Erikson, Erik. *Childhood and Society,* Second Revised Edition. New York: W. W. Norton & Co., 1964.

_____. *Insight and Responsibility.* New York: W.W. Norton & Co., 1964.

Friedman, Edwin. *Generation to Generation.* New York: Guilford Press, 1985.

Gerkin, Charles. *Living Human Document: Revisioning Pastoral Counseling in a Hermeneutical Mode.* Nashville: Abingdon Press, 1984.

Gleason, Jr., John. *Growing Up to God: Eight Steps in Religious Development.* Nashville: Abingdon, 1975.

The Unwanted Gift of Grief: A Ministry Approach
© 2006 by The Haworth Press, Inc. All rights reserved.
doi:10.1300/5644_20

Hart, Archibald. *Overcoming Anxiety*. Dallas: Word Publishing, 1989.

Koenig, Harold G. *The Healing Power of Faith*. New York: Touchstone Books, Simon & Schuster, 1999.

_____. *Spirituality in Patient Care: Why, How, When, and What*. Philadelphia: Templeton Foundation Press, 2002.

Kübler-Ross, Elisabeth. *Death: The Final Stage of Growth*. Engle Cliffs NJ: Prentice Hall, 1975.

Kushner, Harold. *When Bad Things Happen to Good People*. New York: Schocken Books, 1981.

Lester, Andrew. *Hope In Pastoral Care and Counseling*. Louisville, KY: Westminster/John Knox Press, 1995.

_____. *The Angry Christian; A Theology for Care and Counseling*. Louisville, KY: Westminster John Knox Press, 2003

Lewis, C.S. *A Grief Observed*, New York: Bantam Books, 1961.

Manning, Doug. *Don't Take My Grief Away From Me*. Hereford, TX: In-Sight Books, 1983.

Nichols, Michael. *The Lost Art of Listening*. New York: Guilford Press, 1995.

Nouwen, Henri. *The Wounded Healer*. Garden City, NY: Image Books, 1972.

Oates, Wayne. *Grief, Transitions, and Loss: A Pastor's Practical Guide*. Minneapolis: Fortress Press, 1997.

_____. *Your Particular Grief*. Philadelphia: Westminster Press, 1981.

Peck, M. Scott. *The Road Less Traveled*. New York: Simon and Schuster, 1978.

_____. with Waldner, Marilyn & Gay, Patricia. *What Return Can I Make?: Dimensions of the Christian Experience*. New York: Simon and Schuster, 1985.

Sanford, John. *Healing Body and Soul: The Meaning of Illness in the New Testament and in Psychotherapy*. Louisville, KY: Westminster/John Knox, 1992.

Satir, Virginia. *Conjoint Family Therapy*, Third Edition, Revised. Palo Alto, CA: Science and Behavior Books, 1983.

Schiff, H.S. *The Bereaved Parent*. New York: Penguin Books, 1977.

Siegel, Bernie S. *Love, Medicine and Miracles*. New York: Harper and Row, 1986.

_____. *Peace, Love and Healing*. New York: Harper and Row, 1989.

Switzer, David. *The Dynamics of Grief*. Nashville: Abingdon, 1970.

_____. *Minister As Crisis Counselor*. Nashville: Abingdon, 1974.

Tolson, Chester & Koenig, Harold. *The Healing Power of Prayer*. Grand Rapids, MI: Baker Books, 2003.

Viorst, Judith. *Necessary Losses: The Loves, Illusions, Dependencies, and Impossible Expectations That All of Us Have to Give Up in Order to Grow*. New York: Simon and Schuster, 1986.

Westberg, Granger, *Good Grief: A Constructive Approach to the Problem of Loss*. Philadelphia: Fortress Press, Harper & Row, 1971.

Worden, J. William. *Grief Counseling and Grief Therapy*. New York: Springer Publ. Co. 1982.

Index

Acceptance, differences from healing, 116-117
Act people, 26-28, 29
Advance directives, 94
Allowing natural death (AND), 92
Amnesia, 61-63
Anger, frustration and
　as part of journey, 66-68
　　asking why, 66-67
　　expression of, 67, 68
　　positive strength of, 67-68
　as regret, remorse, or guilt, 68-71
　　need to forgive self, 69-70
　　recognition of failure, 68-70
　sojourning, 147-52
　toward others, 71-79
　　clergy, 77-79
　　congregation, 77-79
　　God, 77-79
　　health care team, 76-77
　　one who died, 71-72
　　ones we love, 73-76
　　those who don't listen, 72-73

Beatitudes, 4-5
Benson, Herbert, 81
Borysenko, Joan, 81

Children
　differences in grieving, 30
　differentiation, 47
　loss of, 169-170
　suicide and, 42
Compassionate Friends support group, 50

Complementarity, 174-175
Cultural language, 22-24

Darkness, 55-63
　amnesia, 61-63
　disbelief, 56-61
　dynamics of, 55-56
　shock, 56-61
　sojourning, 143-146
Depression, sadness and, 101-114, 162
　getting help, 113-114
　movement into light and healing, 108-110
　normal parts of healing, 101-108
　　describing wrestle with, 106-107
　　God felt as distant or absent, 107
　　identifying characteristics of depression, 104-105
　　lack of understanding by others, 103-104
　　mysterious gift of, 107-108
　　rushing through or avoiding desert of depression, 105-106
　signs of clinical, 110-112
　sojourning, 159-162
Differentiation, 16-17, 46-51, 120-121
Disbelief, 56-61
Distance escalating cycle, 5-6
Do not resuscitate (DNR) orders, 92, 94
Dossey, Larry, 81

Empathic listening, 139
Empathy, 138
Enmeshment, 46-51
Extroverts, 30-31

Faith, 33-37
    inspirational expressive, 35-36
    inspirational repressive, 35
Family language, 22-24
Feel people, 25, 29
Frustration, and anger, 65-79
    as part of journey, 66-68
        asking why, 66-67
        expression of, 67, 68
        positive strength of, 67-68
    as regret, remorse, or guilt, 68-71
        need to forgive self, 69-70
        recognition of failure, 68-70
    sojourning, 147-52
    toward others, 71-79
        clergy, 77-79
        congregation, 77-79
        God, 77-79
        health care team, 76-77
        one who died, 71-72
        ones we love, 73-76
        those who don't listen, 72-73

Gender models, for grieving, 23-24
Gethsemane, Jesus' prayer in, 86, 88,
        89-90
Glorification, 122
God
    anger toward, 33-37
    contracts with, 82-84, 156
    covenant, 86-90, 155
    as great puppeteer, 70
"God & Health: Is Religion Good
        Medicine? Why Science is
        Starting to Believe in Faith
        and Healing" (Kalb), 82
Good death, 1, 92-93
Grief
    date, 140, 176-178
        definitions, 177
        introduction, 176-177
        steps, 177-178
    differences in, 14, 19-31
        collision of needs, 24
        extroverts, 30-31

Grief, differences in (continued)
        family and culture, 22-24
        gender models, 23-24
        introverts, 30-31
        length of time, 20-22
        pathways, 24-29
    examples, 1-2
    facing pain, 14-15
    factors affecting, 33-51
        differentiation, 46-51
        enmeshment, 46-51
        faith, 33-37
        life cycle and development, 45-46
        need for sojourners, 37-39
        rejection, 40-45
        sudden loss or slow, unfolding
            loss, 39-40
        suicide, 40-45
    as gift, 1, 12-14, 125-126
    as gratitude, 5, 9-11
    as journey of wondering, 17-18
    letting go of past, 15-17
    marriage and, 169-178
        complementarity, 174-175
        couples and grieving, 169-171
        gender differences, 171-174
        guide for couples and family
            members, 176-178
        sexual closeness, 175-176
    professional observation of, 3
    profound, 10
    return of, 129-133
    as roller coaster ride, 4
    talking out pain of, 3
    trying to avoid, 13
    unwanted, 11-12
    ways of making it through, 179-183
    as wilderness, 9-14
    work, 12, 15

Healing, 115-127
    acceptance versus, 116-117
    described, 120-126
        deeper wisdom, humor, and
            spirituality, 125

Healing, described *(continued)*
   grief as unwanted gift, 125-126
   life feels like an invitation again,
     120-121
   living life to the fullest, 122
   need for sojourners and support,
     122-125
   not leaving loved one behind,
     121-122
  euphoria, 118-120
  mysterious spirit of transformation,
    126-127
  sojourning, 163-165
  turning points in wilderness, 116-118

Incarnate love, 138
Interdependence, 47-48
Introverts, 30-31
Involvement, in relationships, 45
Isaiah 40:28-31 RSV, 127

Jesus, prayer in Gethsemane, 86, 88,
   89-90

Kalb, Claudia, 82
Koenig, Harold, 81
Kübler-Ross, Elisabeth, 83

Life After Loss support group, 50
Listening, 138-139, 147-148, 156, 159
Loss
  slow unfolding, 39-40
  sudden, 39-40
  types, 13
Love, 13-14
  incarnate, 138
  need for, 48
  unbonding, 14

Marriage, and grief, 169-178
  complementarity, 174-175
  couples and grieving, 169-171
  gender differences, 171-174
   clarification of, 171-173
   mutuality in grieving, 174
   reconciling different needs, 173
  guide for couples and family
    members, 176-178
  sexual closeness, 175-176
Mathew 5:45 RSV, 155
Mathew 26:39 RSV, 154
McSherry, Elisabeth, 81
Microscopic listening ability, 138
Miracles, praying for, 81-99
  advance directives, 94
  contracts, 82-84
  DNR orders, 92, 94
  example, 94-99
  good death example, 92-93
  good miracle example, 94-99
  saying yes to death and suffering,
    84-92
   belief in a God of covenant, 86-90
   contracts and feelings of
    isolation, inadequacy, and
    guilt, 85-86
   hope for healing and cure, 90-92
  sojourning, 153-157
Mirroring, 145
Mourning, 4-5

On Death and Dying (Kübler-Ross), 83

Parents of Children with Down
    Syndrome, 50
Pathways, through grief, 24-29
  act people, 26-28, 29
  feel people, 25, 29
  strengths, 28-29
  think people, 25, 28
  weaknesses, 28-29

Post-traumatic stress disorder (PTSD),
    62
Prayer, 81-82
Psalm 22, 148, 155-156
Psalm 23, 155
PTSD. *See* post-traumatic stress
    disorder (PTSD)

Reaction formation, 23-24
Rejection, 40-45
Rogers, Carl, 138-139

Sadness, and depression, 101-114, 162
    getting help, 113-114
    movement into light and healing,
        108-110
    normal parts of healing, 101-108
        describing wrestle with, 106-107
        God felt as distant or absent, 107
        identifying characteristics of
            depression, 104-105
        lack of understanding by others,
            103-104
        rushing through or avoiding
            desert of depression, 105-106
    signs of clinical, 110-112
    sojourning, 159-162
"Sermon on the Mount," 4-5
Sexuality, 175-176
Shock, 56-61
    computer, 58-59
    eruption of emotions, 60-61
    "life as always," 56-58

Sojourner, 137-142
    characteristics, 139
    defined, 137-139, 14
    need for, 37-39, 122-125
    process guide, 140-142
        definitions, 140, 141
        introduction, 140
        steps, 141-142
    professionals as, 39
Sojourning
    frustration and anger amid "why?",
        147-152
    praying for a miracle, 153-157
    sadness and depression, 159-162
    unbelievable darkness, 143-146
SOS. *See* Survivors of Suicide (SOS)
Spiritual wrestle, 33-37
Suicidal ideation, 112, 113
Suicide, 40-45
Support
    groups, 49-50
    value of, 49-51
Survivors of Suicide (SOS), 41

Think people, 25, 28
Touch, 144
The Unwanted Gift of Grief
    (VanDuivendyk), 3, 5-6

VanDuivendyk, Tim P., 3, 5-6

Wilderness, of grief. *See* Grief

Order a copy of this book with this form or online at:
http://www.haworthpress.com/store/product.asp?sku=5644

THE UNWANTED GIFT OF GRIEF
A Ministry Approach

_____ in hardbound at $34.95 (ISBN-13: 978-0-7890-2949-2; ISBN-10: 0-7890-2949-9)

_____ in softbound at $14.95 (ISBN-13: 978-0-7890-2950-8; ISBN-10: 0-7890-2950-2)

188 pages plus index

Or order online and use special offer code HEC25 in the shopping cart.

COST OF BOOKS_____

POSTAGE & HANDLING_____
(US: $4.00 for first book & $1.50
for each additional book)
(Outside US: $5.00 for first book
& $2.00 for each additional book)

SUBTOTAL_____

IN CANADA: ADD 7% GST_____

STATE TAX_____
(NJ, NY, OH, MN, CA, IL, IN, PA, & SD
residents, add appropriate local sales tax)

FINAL TOTAL_____
(If paying in Canadian funds,
convert using the current
exchange rate, UNESCO
coupons welcome)

☐ **BILL ME LATER:** (Bill-me option is good on
US/Canada/Mexico orders only; not good to
jobbers, wholesalers, or subscription agencies.)
☐ Check here if billing address is different from
shipping address and attach purchase order and
billing address information.

Signature_____

☐ **PAYMENT ENCLOSED: $_____**

☐ **PLEASE CHARGE TO MY CREDIT CARD.**

☐ Visa ☐ MasterCard ☐ AmEx ☐ Discover
☐ Diner's Club ☐ Eurocard ☐ JCB

Account #_____

Exp. Date_____

Signature_____

Prices in US dollars and subject to change without notice.

NAME_____

INSTITUTION_____

ADDRESS_____

CITY_____

STATE/ZIP_____

COUNTRY_____ COUNTY (NY residents only)_____

TEL_____ FAX_____

E-MAIL_____

May we use your e-mail address for confirmations and other types of information? ☐ Yes ☐ No
We appreciate receiving your e-mail address and fax number. Haworth would like to e-mail or fax special
discount offers to you, as a preferred customer. **We will never share, rent, or exchange your e-mail address
or fax number.** We regard such actions as an invasion of your privacy.

Order From Your Local Bookstore or Directly From
The Haworth Press, Inc.
10 Alice Street, Binghamton, New York 13904-1580 • USA
TELEPHONE: 1-800-HAWORTH (1-800-429-6784) / Outside US/Canada: (607) 722-5857
FAX: 1-800-895-0582 / Outside US/Canada: (607) 771-0012
E-mail to: orders@haworthpress.com

For orders outside US and Canada, you may wish to order through your local
sales representative, distributor, or bookseller.
For information, see http://haworthpress.com/distributors

(Discounts are available for individual orders in US and Canada only, not booksellers/distributors.)
PLEASE PHOTOCOPY THIS FORM FOR YOUR PERSONAL USE.
http://www.HaworthPress.com   BOF06